T0197260

'This book is like having an academic mentor in your pocket. It is a book that will stay with you, ready to be pulled off a shelf or out of a bag at a moment's notice. You can dip into it any time a little guidance is needed or when you need to be reminded of what you are doing or why you are doing it. Les' book offers a steadying, supportive and reassuring voice in the chaos. Compassion and vitality spring from the pages, fostering an enduring spring of solidarity in the reader. I would go as far as saying that all academics should make sure that they have a copy to hand.'

David Beer, Reader in Sociology, University of York

'When discussions of higher education in England are dominated by loans and questions of finance, it's all too easy to forget about the lived, transformative experience of education. Episodes in *Academic Diary* serve as healthy reminders of what ought to be central to universities and colleges: learning. More than that, Les Back's generosity and collegiality forge the politics of this book into something distinct. Walter Benjamin wrote in his commentaries on Bertolt Brecht: "Whoever wants to make the hard thing give way should miss no opportunity for friendliness." In a similar spirit, *Academic Diary* tempers sentiment with critical aims.'

Andrew McGettigan, author of *The Great University Gamble: Money, Markets and the Future of Higher Education*

'Inaugurating the exciting arrival of Goldsmiths Press, Les Back's *Academic Diary* reminds us of the exigency of writing large the small and intricate matters of the academy now. At once a comforting and challenging read, I only hope that Back's example will inspire yet more loving experimentation in listening and being heard; and more courageous presses ready to take up the challenge of carrying diverse intellectual voices.'

Elspeth Probyn, Professor of Gender and Cultural Studies, University of Sydney

'Against the cynicism and despair of so much discourse on the contemporary university, here is a beautifully-written book, full of reflection and reverie, decency and front-line documentation, that addresses the challenges of teaching in an increasingly market-oriented profession, but also celebrates the persistent mysteries, necessary anarchy and – yes – pleasures of the classroom.'

Sukhdev Sandhu, Director of the Colloquium for Unpopular Culture, New York University

'Just when you might have thought that a combination of Gradgrind assessment, bullying managerialism, and crass marketization had ripped the heart and soul out of British higher education, along comes the admirable Les Back with this profoundly humanistic account of the unexpected and often fleeting day-to-day pleasures of working in a contemporary university.

Whether he is discussing the plight of increasingly indebted students or the unacknowledged endeavours of the non-academic staff who make universities work or the tribulations of overseas students attempting to overcome the indignities of ever-harsher border controls, Back displays a generosity of spirit and an alertness to the pulse and feel of everyday life outside the campus gates which stands in stark contrast to the mean-minded individualistic scholasticism that is rapidly becoming the signature mark of the modern academic.'

Laurie Taylor, Broadcaster and former Professor of Sociology, University of York

Les Back is Professor of Sociology at Goldsmiths, University of London. He received a PhD in Social Anthropology from Goldsmiths and taught previously at the Department of Cultural Studies, University of Birmingham. His books include *The Art of Listening* and *The Auditory Culture Reader* (with Michael Bull) and *The Changing Face of Football: Racism, Identity and Multiculture in the English Game* (with Tim Crabbe and John Solomos). He writes journalism and has made documentary films and lives in south London.

Academic Diary

Or Why Higher Education
Still Matters

Les Back

Goldsmiths
Press

Published in 2016
by Goldsmiths Press
Goldsmiths, University of London, New Cross
London SE14 6NW

Distribution by The MIT Press
Cambridge, Massachusetts, and London, England

A CIP record for this book
is available from the British Library

ISBN 978-1-906-89758-1 (pbk)
ISBN 978-1-906-89757-4 (ebk)

www.gold.ac.uk/goldsmiths-press

In memory of
David Finch

Contents

Introduction:
Academic Time

An academic diary provides the time frame of university life: it also gives it a storyline. Early September marks the beginning of another year. Jay Parini says that academic life is renewed with the fall of autumn leaves, 'shredding the previous year's failures and tossing them out of the window like so much confetti'. It is a time to plan the year ahead. The academic diary is also a navigation device, a compass ensuring – as far as possible – that we are in the right place (meetings, lectures, seminars) at the right time.

Written in the form of a chronicle, this book comprises a series of short essays that take the form of diary entries. Each reflects the seasons of faculty existence located within what Elaine Showalter calls 'academic time'. It isn't a specific year but rather the accumulation of thirty years of reflection on the university and scholarship as both student and teacher, presented as a single year. Organized into three main seasons – autumn, spring and summer – the book tries to chronicle a sense of passing but repeated time in a life of learning.

Why write a book in the form of an academic diary? Isn't it a bit old fashioned in the age of the iPad to bother with a diary? Maybe so. But in a way, the diary symbolizes something ancient and profound about the rhythm and content of an intellectual vocation. As I assembled these stories written over two decades, clear seasonal patterns started to emerge. The diary form became a device to signal the tasks we fill up our diaries with as well as the tempo of academic life ranging from frantic busyness to quiet reflection. To the outsider, the cloistered world of the university can seem full of eccentricity and intrigue. For the uninitiated newcomer, campus life seems governed by absurd invisible protocols and mysterious unwritten rules. The diary aims to demystify them.

Our tale starts in September with graduation – the New Year's Eve of academic life – a time when the fruits of university education are brought to life through the successes of our students. For a university teacher, the period before teaching starts is a period of anxious expectation. For faculty, before the beginning of teaching there is real academic excitement but also a tight-chested dread. They know the intensity of the teaching term is exhausting and by the eighth week they will be saying to their colleagues 'just holding on for the end of term'. As the promises of September wane and the hopefulness of graduation fades, entries segue into the wintry seriousness of topics focused on the autumn term. Each entry addresses an important issue, ranging from teaching and advice to new students to widening participation initiatives and the professional ethics of anonymous peer reviewing.

Spring is a time when changes are afoot and when academic plots are hatched. As Richard Russo writes, 'April is the month of heightened paranoia for academics... Whatever dirt will be done to us is always planned in April.' For this reason the entries in this section focus on the intrigues of academic life from issues such as intellectual recognition, peer reviewing and the auditing of academic value. The spring is when the serious work of teaching is done and when students have to complete assessments. It's also a time when students can run into difficulties as the serious business of revision, dissertation completion and the summer exams starts to loom on the horizon. Easter is also 'conference season' and when papers are given it's possible to meet one's intellectual heroes and adversaries. All these issues are treated in entries for this period.

Summer is the denouement of the academic year. This section of the diary covers exams, invigilation, the stresses of marking and the annual exam board. It is also the period when PhDs have to be completed and vivas planned. By mid-July the academic cycle enters the languid pursuits of late summer when books are authored, articles written and holidays taken.

I also hope that the reflections offered in the pages that follow are useful as a way of orienting the reader in relation to the values of higher education as a place to think together. It does not aspire to the dreary instrumentalism of a 'how to succeed in academia' self-help book. Entries aim to entertain but also to explore intellectual craft, techniques in lecturing, how to supervise PhD students, the challenges of developing one's own writing style, balancing campus responsibilities with engaged research, dealing with the colleagues who constantly 'name drop' or exploring what happens when you meet writers you admire. At the same time, the diary offers a commentary on the quality of higher education and its relationship to the wider world and how it is being disfigured by cultures of audit and commercialization. In these small tales of campus life a larger argument is made for the value of thinking and why university education still matters.

So to begin and our story opens with graduation. It might seem strange to start here, at the end of the student's journey. I have always felt that graduation is really the start of something, the beginning of a new chapter in the student's life but also a moment of renewal for the university and its staff.

Autumn Term

Graduation

For those steeped in academic time, the year's end is in September not December. In my college this coincides with the graduation ceremonies that seem always to be blessed with the last days of bright summer weather. They are the culmination of what are for many students the fullest, most formative and intense years of their life. A period packed with experiences that will be defining. 'I can't believe how fast it's gone' is a common refrain that captures both the student's sense of accelerated time but also a period of rapid intellectual growth. At the exam board we call it 'exit velocity' – that is, students whose marks have increased dramatically in their final year. On graduation day even the most down at heart professor can't help but be reminded of how much distance – intellectually and personally – each student has travelled. The evidence is paraded in front of us as we hear their names read out loud and watch them each in turn take the stage to receive symbolically their degree. There is something vitalizing, for students and faculty alike, about the grandeur of graduation; it's the New Year's Eve of the academic calendar.

It is a good moment to take stock, make resolutions and re-imagine what the university might be. Elaine Showalter comments in her book *Faculty Towers*: 'In the University there are two stories – those of the faculty and those of the students.' She argues that on most campuses in the UK and the US students are happy and satisfied, sometimes 'deliriously so' as she puts it. The achievements of graduation day would appear to support this, despite the burden of student debt and uncertain employment prospects.

It is also a moment to apprehend how much an institution like Goldsmiths has changed. As they are read aloud from the ceremonial platform the names of the graduands echo connections to almost every corner of the world. The 'multicultural drift', which has accompanied both the internationalization of the university and widening access to higher education, to my mind is progress, albeit uneven in terms of inclusiveness and compromised by new borders. The scrutiny of overseas students by the Home Office casts a shadow over the internationalism of today's university, where overseas students are treated as itinerant cash cows passing through UK higher education or, worse, mistrusted potential terrorists.

The impact of the contraction of places as a result of public sector cuts threatens to slow the drift to a more inclusive university. Regardless, the university is valuable now because it provides a place to encounter and live with differences and think beyond national horizons. This rarely produces clashes between immutable cultural blocks – although it can sometimes – but more routinely it involves exploring perspectives that shift, histories that are debates and cultures animated through the interplay between the legacy of the past and their emergent new forms in the present. While campus life is still haunted by racism, increasingly it strikes me that what is on display on graduation day is a vital and productive diversity. Bill Readings refers to it as a 'community of dissensus' where disagreement or a lack of consensus is productive because it drives us to think harder about the key issues and problems of our time.

Higher education is valuable because it enables students to learn to live in a world saturated with information. We are bombarded with data, words and images which transforms not only what counts as knowledge but also the reality of our own existence. Susan Sontag noted that those who witnessed firsthand the World Trade Center bombings on 11 September 2001 described what they saw as 'unreal' and 'like a movie', while those of us around the globe who watched the devastation in real time on our television screens experienced it as a hyper-reality. Seeing the towers fall in New York seemed less real than the distant view on TV. The university is a place to prepare students for a life in such a society, to learn how information mediates the way we understand ourselves and our place in the world. It is where we learn how to judge between fabricated realities and distinguish them from our most intimate and profound personal commitments.

What then of 'The Faculty', Elaine Showalter's second campus story in *Faculty Towers*? Using the academic novel as a kind of social barometer, Showalter argues that the mood among staff stands in stark contrast to that of students. The scholarly idyll captured in C.P. Snow's *The Masters* is replaced with a joyless atmosphere of rivalry, pettiness, malevolence, anxiety and status obsession. Today's academic novels might not correspond to how life is on campus but they do convey, in exaggerated form, elements of the faculty imagination. 'Vocation has become employment; critics have become superstars; scholars have become technicians,' summarizes Showalter. There is also a sense of being beleaguered by the changing priorities and systems that aim to audit scholarly value. The pressure to publish, the confidence-withering hierarchies of what is deemed 'cutting edge' or academically worthy all contribute to a kind of extreme vocational anxiety. I would add silencing, timidity and conservatism to Showalter's list of faculty pathos and downheartedness.

Graduation

In a modest way this diary is an attempt to point to alternative choices and add other tales. If graduation is the university's New Year's Eve then it is an apt moment to reflect on the version of academic life we aspire to and hope for. 'New Year is the annual festivity marking the resurrection of hopes,' writes Bauman. For him this includes a 'meta-hope', or what he calls the 'mother of all hopes'. On New Year's Eve there is the promise that our hopes will not be dashed. Bauman says this is summed up in the feeling that: 'This time it will end differently, this time our hopes will be made flesh and brought to life . . .'

As tenured bystanders we feel the vicarious sense of rejuvenation from simply being at the annual festivity of graduation. It is a moment to insist that another kind of university is possible and to resolve to act in a way to make it so. Apocalyptic portrayals of the demise of the university as a place to think are cold comfort for they offer few clues as to how one might act as an academic writer and teacher.

Ros Gill has argued that the neoliberal university, with its individualization of performance and value, results in a peculiarly toxic environment that is suffered secretly and silently. 'Neoliberalism found fertile ground in academics whose predispositions to "work hard" and "do well" meshed perfectly with its demands for autonomous, self-motivating, responsibilized subjects,' she argues. Here worthy characteristics like scholarly dedication and the ambition to do good work merge seamlessly with neoliberal imperatives based on egotism and selfishness. The overwhelming experience of 'fast academia' is pressure, self-exploitation (which can mean putting off or sacrificing the personal fulfilment of having children, particularly for women), vituperative meanness and toxic shame. Our most deeply held values of engaged work, careful thought and creativity become cruel promises because the conditions to realize them are no longer possible. If the university is in ruins, as Bill Readings has suggested, how is it possible to carry on with an intellectual vocation?

The quick pessimistic answer is to say it isn't possible: the forms of auditing, professionalization and managerialism have dealt the university a fatal blow. I think we have to find a way to resist these shifts, loosen the grip of self-regulation and act differently. Reading back through these pages I realize my own answers are hidden in the detail of each of the entries. What do these moral tales add up to, what kind of academic vocation is advocated in them? Before ending I want to try to formulate an answer through proposing a series of key principles. The first of these is to slow thinking down – be it theoretical or practical – and to value the time it takes. It entails the cultivation of the capacity for judicious speech and crafted attentiveness.

The overwhelming bureaucratic impulse to speed up academic production, and make academics into tacticians preoccupied with the game of professional standing, results in a concern with short-term gains. As a result the books and articles we write are destined to have a short shelf life. To combat this I think it is important to try to resist the temptation to think too fast and write too much, too quickly. It doesn't mean encouraging PhD students to languish for decades without completing their PhDs, or sitting on manuscripts that will never be read. A balance needs to be struck between the progression of a piece of research or a book and taking time to think and write, so that what we produce has a lasting quality.

Secondly, we need to take risks in order to expand not only what can be thought but also what counts as academic writing and communication. It means also aspiring to be a communicator of ideas not just on campus or within the pages of academic journals but in a wide variety of public and educational arenas. Thirdly, we need to see that what we do is not just a job but an intellectual vocation or craft.

Specialization and professionalization institutionalize narrowness and result paradoxically in anti-intellectualism. Being a slave to specialism is self-confinement: 'I can only talk about "my own area of expertise".' It promotes individualism in that we academics become conservative with our time and shut ourselves away in our offices or become campus absentees. Perhaps lessening the hold of the imperious specialist on the university might result in cutting academic vanity and self-importance down to size. The last and most important principle is to value teaching and to see the university primarily as a place of learning.

It is absurd in a way that we have arrived at a point where such an argument is even necessary. A university without students is a contradiction in terms. One of the privileges of being an academic is that we have the power to frame what happens in the classroom and the intellectual values we communicate as we perform this role. The investments and care taken in the context of teaching – from the first-year introductory lecture or a PhD supervision session – involve developing both an ethics of thinking and what Max Weber called 'the tools and training for thought'. Teaching a course creates a community of thought and a space for dialogue and reflection. Here students struggle to understand not only the 'learning outcomes' but where they are in the mix of history and the world around them and how to form their own judgements in a society saturated with information.

Everyone Has a Teacher Story

It will seem odd – I am sure – but I still feel a shudder of anxiety when receiving an invitation to an academic dinner or function. It's the informality of these occasions that still throws me even after more than twenty years. Perhaps it is a lingering trace of the awkward 18-year-old Goldsmiths student, who, when offered a cup of Earl Grey tea in the first week by his hall of residence neighbour, said he thought the milk was off! So, when I received an invitation to attend the Fellows' Dinner – a large black-tie banquet held at Goldsmiths to celebrate the award of honorary degrees at graduation – it provoked a discomforting feeling, as if I were already wearing the ill-fitting suit that I would need to dust off for the occasion.

This was all worry for no reason of course. When I arrived at the dinner I saw to my delight I was placed at a table with anti-racist campaigner Doreen Lawrence and Marxist geographer David Harvey – both had received honorary degrees this year. Also, sitting next to me was one of my favourite Goldsmiths colleagues, Natalie Fenton, Professor of Media Studies and one of the key figures in the 'Hacked Off' campaign against journalistic abuses. Sitting next to me on the other side was Professor Harvey's date for the evening, a wonderful woman called Jane Shallice. Jane explained that she is a teacher and had worked in London for many years. She told great stories of school life but also of her increasing dismay at government policy on education and the damage it was doing.

Jane asked me about my own experience of schooling and how I had ended up going to university. I explained that I had a special teacher. I guess 'everyone has a teacher story', I remember saying. Mine was my form tutor who had chosen to work in a large comprehensive school in Croydon for political reasons. He had a real sense of humour. I explained that when I was studying the Russian revolution he loaned me a beautiful boxed edition of Trotsky's multi-volume history. Almost startled, Jane said: 'You don't mean Dave Finch, do you?' I nodded and said, 'Yes, that's right.' She paused, then with sadness on her face continued: 'I am really sorry to tell you but Dave died in February.' It was devastating news.

Although we had not spoken for a while, Dave and I had been in regular contact. We started to meet again after he had read something I had written in The Guardian newspaper criticizing the government's immigration policy that promoted an atmosphere of racism. He emailed me and it was the first contact I had with him for almost fifteen years. I remember the conversation we had on the phone after he had read the article. He said approvingly, 'Glad to hear you haven't changed your accent much.' He subsequently came to my inaugural lecture at Goldsmiths in 2005 that marked my promotion to Professor of Sociology. Always the teacher, he playfully offered his critique afterwards and encouraged me to be more politically forthright.

When asked his age Dave Finch liked to say that he was born in Stoke Newington 'three years after the Russian revolution'. He was one of six children of Jewish immigrants from Poland and Ukraine. His father made fur coats and his mother was a machinist. Like many Jewish working-class households in the thirties, political arguments were standard fare at the dinner table. He told me these ranged from the latest news from Russia to the execution of anarchists Sacco and Vanzetti in the United States in 1927. Education was his way of creating a new kind of life and he attended University College London where he studied chemistry.

In 1943 he joined the newly formed Trotskyist Revolutionary Communist Party linked to the Fourth International. After the war Dave decided to join the Labour Party as part of an organized revolutionary faction aimed at changing the party from within. The leadership at the time decided that the activists should get closer to the working class. Dave and several others were sent off to become miners in Cannock, where they quickly became organizers of the pit committee. After a mining accident in which Dave was injured he came back to London and he returned to chemistry. Between 1948 and 1952 he worked as an industrial chemist at Deptford power station. He was 'eased out' – as he put it – by his boss, who was an active Tory, and didn't like him talking to the apprentices about politics.

Anger about the injustices at the heart of class-divided society stayed with Dave all his life. But he was not an angry man. Rather he was a charming rogue – particularly in the company of women – able to make a political point or an educational observation with a laugh and a joke. In the 1960s Dave switched tack again to pursue a new career, this time in teaching. At John Newnham High School – where I met him – he taught science and he was particularly active in the National Union of Teachers.

People in Croydon used to joke – sometimes derisively – about Dave Finch and 'The People's Republic of John Newnham'. My father – who worked in factories all his life – loved him; Dave was never condescending to the working-class parents who came to the school, although he was often quite searching in his criticism of them. But comments like 'you know your son should really be doing better in Chemistry' were always delivered with a wry and knowing smile. With 'Finchy' you might have to listen to a few home truths but you accepted them from him because in some deep way you realized he understood your world.

Dave didn't teach me much chemistry, although I wonder sometimes whether my fascination with the writings of Primo Levi – the Italian chemist and Auschwitz survivor – is not in some way linked to him. Through lending me his personal copies of Friedrich Engels' *Origin of the Family Private Property and The State* he taught me a deep lesson about fostering a love of books and ideas.

For example, he loaned me a book by Tom Wintringham called *Mutiny* which had a really strong impact on me; I can still feel its blue canvas cover and those pages yellowed by time. The book is a survey of mutinies throughout history from the Spartacus slave rebellion to the Invergordon mutiny of 1931. Wintringham showed that in each case their history had been revised and the facts changed. These were books not on the official curriculum, but Dave introduced me to their magic and also to critical scepticism. Things are 'not what they seem', he would always say.

Dave taught me that it is important for teachers to pass on a love and an excitement for reading and that the gift of a book can plant a seed in the life of its recipient. I wish there had been one last opportunity to thank him for this bequest. I think he knew though all along. My guess is he would have made light of it and laughed off such a weighty expression of gratitude.

Nevertheless, I feel the force of his example every time I find myself pulling a book off the shelf, handing it to a student saying, 'Read this – it will help you understand. Things are not what they seem.'

Letter to a New Student

A friend asked recently: 'You work in a university, what advice would you give to a new student like Hannah?' His daughter is preparing to start a course at the University of Sheffield. Poring over decisions such as what things to take to 'uni', Hannah is also imagining what it will be like to leave home and begin her degree course. My first thought was to admit that perhaps I am actually not the best person. The student experience today is fundamentally different from what it was thirty years ago when I was in Hannah's position.

One of the dangers of being a university teacher is of losing touch with the memory of what it meant to be a student. Students today not only pay to study, they work while they learn. Chatting to a current third-year student while she served me in the college bookshop, I asked her if she thought about further study after her degree. 'I'd like to do an MA . . . but I'd have to save up first.' It really shocked me. Of course, that's how students have to think. There is something deeply humbling in the thirst that young people have for learning regardless of its cost. Anyway, I am stalling. This is for you, Hannah, and new students anywhere who are thinking nervously about the prospects of university life.

Letter to a New Student

1. Listen but don't be silent

In the early part of the twentieth century, philosopher Friedrich Nietzsche gave a series of lectures on the future of educational institutions. In his fifth lecture Nietzsche imagines a foreign visitor trying to make sense of academic study. The visitor asks how are students connected with the university, what is their point of connection to thinking and knowledge. The narrator in Nietzsche's parable responds: 'By the ear, as a hearer.' The lecture continues but the visitor is astonished and asks again: surely listening isn't the only way that a student is connected to learning. Nietzsche's professor reiterates that undergraduates are connected to the university: 'Only by the ear... The student hears.'

Much of the architecture of higher learning is dedicated to reinforcing the image of Nietzsche's obediently silent student. Students sit in row after row of seats all directed toward the stage and the lectern. It is also impossible to have a proper group discussion in a lecture theatre – they are designed for monologues, not dialogues. Nikolas Rose once told me of a session he would do at the beginning of the academic year that tried to make this authority structure explicit. He would turn up to a large first-year lecture in sociology, take to the stage, open his file of notes and place them on the lectern. He would look down at his notes but say absolutely nothing! Often latecomers would arrive apologetically with umbrellas after being soaked by an autumn shower. Someone near the front would say, 'It's alright – he hasn't started yet.' They found their seats. The expectant students waited silently, pens poised, for Nikolas to say something. He said nothing. One year he managed to say nothing for forty minutes.

When the excruciating silence was eventually broken he would use it to explore how it could be understood sociologically. The ordering of speaking and listening is part of the social furniture of the lecture hall and Nikolas would invite students to think about the way power, authority and knowledge were implicated in what had unfolded that morning. I doubt it was a lecture any of his students ever forgot.

Nietzsche captures something important. Higher learning means that students have to train their ears. It is increasingly hard in our world of distractions to listen with undivided attention for a whole hour. Via mobile phones we hold the world in the palm of our hand and the temptation to text and email under the table is particularly strong. Many educators believe that the kind of obedient listening that takes place in a lecture is actually not a very good way to learn at all. I am sure this is right. However, a lecture is a listening workout. It forces students to face the difficulties of training a deep attentiveness.

It is unsurprising then that students find it hard to speak out, ask questions or for points of clarification when they don't understand. They don't want to appear foolish or incapable. So, Hannah, listen attentively but don't be silenced by the authority structure of the lecture hall. There is no such thing as a foolish question. It is the teacher's job to help you understand. This also goes for seminars and workshops. Regardless of the heavy historical weight of academic authority, every lecturer's worst nightmare is a group of students who will not speak. So train your ear, listen carefully, but don't be silent.

2. Care about your grades but don't make them your only goal
Education in English schools has become so bureaucratic, obsessed with targets and levels of achievement, that pupils talk about their understanding within a grid of levels almost without reference to content. 'I am a level 6b in maths and I need to be a 7a,' says the concerned Key Stage 3 student. The substance of what is learned has become almost irrelevant. This is having a carry-over effect on undergraduate students who have become increasingly instrumental in their relation-

ship to learning. 'What do I have to do to get a 2.1 in your class?' The truth is that it just doesn't work like that.

There is no straightforward correspondence between how much you put into an assignment and the final grade. Of course, working hard, reading widely, following advice and guidance all help keep you on track. Write on topics that are genuinely interesting to you. Have ambition to understand as much as you can, submit yourself to the craft of thinking and focus on the content first and the grade second. This is actually the best way to ensure that you achieve the highest assessment levels.

3. Read and buy books

If instrumentalism leads to grade obsession then it also limits students' engagement with reading. Reading is the most important thing that any student does. There are so many online sources today that are useful to students but the habit of reading books – whole books – is something that is being lost. Students often come into my study and say, 'God, you've got lots of books, have you read them all?' 'Yes, most of them,' I reply. 'They are the fundamental tools of the trade and they are the tools of your trade too.'

Buy your own books. There are many bargains to be found on used-book websites or through the dubious magic of Amazon. Seek out second-hand bookshops where you can find things in your area of interest. Buy books.

I remember when I was a student I found an early twentieth-century dictionary in a local used bookshop. It has a wonderful glossary of Latin phrases, proverbs, maxims and mottoes. I still use it. Every time I need to look up a word for its precise meaning I mark it with a pencil. After thirty years of these marks the dictionary is like a record of my education. This is partly why having books is so important: because we leave an imprint of ourselves and our reading eye in them through our scribbles and the passages that we highlight or underline.

There are essentially two kinds of book lovers. There are 'vandals' like myself who deface the printed page with marginalia, intelligent graffiti that either refute or applaud. Then there are 'preservationists' who jealously protect the virgin pages of their books from defilement. Being a book lover and buyer will help any student get the most out of their education regardless of which camp they end up in.

4. Don't try and do it all the night before

As a student, you don't just have to learn to listen and become a critical reader, you also have to become an academic writer. I often say to students that the story of a degree begins with learning how to consume and read critically the books in the field of study, but ends with them becoming producers and writers of sociology. The short version of what I want to say is that this cannot be done in a rush the night before. Resist the temptation to cut and paste passages from the internet or to copy sections from books. You'll hear a lot about plagiarism in the course of your degree. Universities are unforgiving and have almost criminalized copying. In most cases, students who plagiarize do it out of desperation or because it is a shortcut when they are running out of time.

Last year a student came to see me. She wanted to talk about a paper that she had written for my course. She had received a very low mark, barely passed. The grade at this point was provisional because the papers were due to be sent to the external examiner to be evaluated. She looked at her hands in her lap as she sat down, avoiding eye contact. 'What happened?' I asked. 'I am so ashamed and disappointed in myself and I am sorry,' she said. 'I did it the night before – just to get something in.' I told her that all that was left was to try to learn from the experience.

Letter to a New Student

The external examiner looked at the paper and insisted – rightly – that it had been marked too leniently and failed it. I am always reluctant to fail students. As our department administrator commented, 'Les, you are not doing them any favours by letting it pass when it shouldn't.' She was of course right. Former Warden Richard Hoggart reflected in his memoir: 'Goldsmiths' weakness grew directly out of its good will. It hated to close its doors to anyone; it agonized even more than is usual about possible examination failures; it rallied to any member in difficulties; it often made judgements more with the heart than the head.' I realized that I'd fallen foul of this well-intentioned vice.

Time passed and before long the summer re-sits came around. A package of papers arrived via the internal mail to be marked including the re-sit from the student mentioned here. The paper was unrecognizable – thoughtful, informed, well written. I graded it as a high 2.1 before realizing who had written it. When the results were announced a very different student came to see me. Her face bright and animated, she said, 'I worked really hard on it and in the end I was really proud of what I did. Showed myself that I can really do this.' Her mark was capped at 50 because of the initial failure but the essay was considerably better than the bare pass. I had learned something too. I had been wrong to pass it and if the external examiner hadn't insisted on dropping the grade the student would have been denied the opportunity to try again. In many respects re-writing the assessment has proved to be the turning point in her degree and her whole university education. She's no longer a failing student.

Written work at this level cannot be done at the last minute or in a rush. It takes time. Use your teachers: if they will read draft essays then make sure you can get feedback on them ahead of the final submission. If they won't read drafts then go and see them to run through your ideas. Students who get feedback on their work always do better than those who do not. It is one of the few educational laws that holds true in all cases.

5. Don't be just a consumer

'I need to get the most out of this because I am paying for it,' I overhear a first year say to her friend as she dashes to an induction meeting. The marketization of the university has turned campuses into places of commerce. It corrodes the value of thinking and learning. Money can't buy a thought, or a connection between ideas or things, or a link between a private trouble and a public issue. The idea that education promises a straightforward return on a financial outlay reduces thought to a commodity. The commercialization of higher education cheapens us all. It is entirely logical that students should start to see themselves as paying customers. I think it is incumbent on staff to make their teaching worth the price it has cost.

Students need to be offered an environment for learning and if that's not forthcoming they should demand it to be so. 'The more it costs, the less it's worth,' students shouted in protest to the introduction of fees and indebtedness. Nevertheless, thinking and intellectual growth cannot be purchased 'off the peg'. It makes universities into places of skills transmission or a kind of financial transaction. The university can foster a place where we can 'think together' about difficult problems and practise what Fichte called the 'exercise of critical judgement'. This means not being just a consumer and thinking for yourself with others.

6. Follow your interests

One last thing, Hannah – it is important to get involved in things outside the seminar room or the lecture theatre. I know it's harder now because students have to work as well as study. But get involved in the student societies, or the student newspaper or things going on locally in terms of campaigns, or be active in the student union. Those things can be life-defining, the beginning of something that will be important for the rest of your life. It's true for people I've known.

When I was a student there was a guy in the year below me called Rob Stringer. He studied sociology. He was a truly awful student – shocking, by his own admission. Rob loved music and partying and as an extension of his twin passions he was elected the student union social sec. He organized gigs and events but being involved in the union was the start of something for him. He went on to work in the record business initially as an A&R (artists and repertoire) person developing new acts. Now he's very high up in Sony/BMG and one of the most powerful figures in the music industry. But it all began for him in the Goldsmiths Union. It doesn't matter if you think working for Sony is a good or a bad thing, what matters, I think, is realizing that really useful knowledge can be learned in all sorts of places and not just found on your course reading lists.

Finally, let me try and sum up. Take time to read, think and doubt. Ask questions and get feedback. The time invested is never wasted because you are investing in learning to think for yourself. This will give you more than just good grades: it will help you establish your own commitments and bearing in life. Make sure that you attend all your lectures and seminars and be present in them physically and intellectually. Many students just don't turn up even though the cost to them is high financially and academically. Listen hard and with care but don't be gagged by the seeming grandeur of clever people. It shouldn't take long to see that even the most brilliant lecturer is in fact all too human with the same weaknesses and foibles as anyone else.

Welcome Week

Just a few weeks after graduation the new intake of students arrives for induction or what used to be called 'Freshers' and is now re-titled 'Welcome Week'. In London this coincides with cold but sunny mornings that mark the beginning of autumn, although its effect has yet to strip the leaves from the trees. These bright days are cherished because just a few weeks away is the dreary mid-term winter when it will be dark at 5 p.m. For now the 'first years' have the institution to themselves. The college is a maze. They are continually getting lost, finding their way with smiling nervousness through trial and error.

Induction marks the beginning of something significant, even though it is impossible to know exactly what has begun. Eavesdropping on the awkward introductions and the chance meetings is enchanting because we know from our own experience that some of the friendships started here will prove to be life-long, through good times and dark moments. Others will be broken by an imbalance of give and take or some future conflict that is unimaginable now. It is a time of beginnings and resurrected hopes, as staff and students alike contemplate the curriculum and peel back the fresh pages of a new diary.

Goldsmiths and its District

Goldsmiths is the closest university to the place where I was born. I studied here as an undergraduate and postgraduate student and have taught at Goldsmiths for most of my professional life. I am sure you've already come to the conclusion that I evidently don't really like the place very much!

Mine is a personal story affectionately written about the place in which it is set. Richard Hoggart was the Warden of the college when I first came to Goldsmiths in 1981. He had taken up this position because for him Goldsmiths still had the trace of what he called the 'Great Tradition' of adult education with its roots in the nineteenth-century institutions like the Worker's Education Association. The college takes its name from a medieval City Guild called the Goldsmiths Company, which established the Goldsmiths Institute in 1891. The gold and silver hallmarking on jewellery is provided for a fee by this ancient guild and it validates Britain's currency as well for other countries. Almost from its inception The Company gave money to support crafts and educational philanthropy. London's impoverished southeast corner was a fitting place to concentrate its investment.

Hoggart – the author of the classic study of working-class life *The Uses of Literacy* – chose Goldsmiths over prestigious offers in more auspicious places. In the late seventies and early eighties New Cross and Deptford on the south bank of the Thames were ruined by de-industrialization, dock closures resulting from containerization and urban decline. As sociologist Dick Hobbs has pointed out, between 1966 and 1976 150,000 jobs were lost in London's dockland communities. Hoggart wrote in his memoir that the 'district' – as he used to refer to the college's surrounding areas – is commonly known as 'the arsehole of London'.

The Goldsmiths ethos of openness and accessibility enticed Hoggart to southeast London, which was close to his vision of why education mattered. Hoggart, a working-class scholarship boy himself from Hunslet, Yorkshire, had cut his teeth as an extra-mural teacher in Hull. The combination of degree courses and open access evening classes offered at Goldsmiths was particularly appealing to him. During the day, the college was home to 18–21-year-old students that came from all over Britain, but at night thousands of local students attended adult education classes here. This part of London also provided a home for post-war colonial citizen migrants largely from Jamaica and the small Caribbean islands of St Lucia, Barbados and St Kitts. The same year that I moved to New Cross, over a dozen young black Londoners died in a racist arson attack during a house party.

I think the sense and feel of the place at that time is best captured by Hoggart when he writes:

> Goodwill breathed from the bricks of the building . . . all the intense vitality you felt the moment you crossed the threshold in the crowd, saw the tattered linoleum, smelled cheap but largely unattractive food and heard the gabble – all this made Goldsmiths a place people either loved or hated . . . If they disliked it they tried to leave soon. If they loved it, if it felt immediately right, they stayed and worked far beyond the call of duty.

Goldsmiths and its District

I stayed. Today Goldsmiths and its 'district' is in some ways a very different place. The 'congenitally shabby' main building that Hoggart describes so aptly has been renovated and renamed in his honour. New migrants from West Africa have settled in this part of London along with others from Latin America, transforming its sounds, tastes and smells. The first signs of gentrification have also started to show – unthinkable thirty years ago – as coffee shops, hipster bars and even organic food delis sprout in the midst of the area's urban ruins. Suited and booted property sharks appear in online promotional videos extolling 'unrivalled investment opportunities' in Deptford as urban grit is transformed into lucrative arty glamour.

The fact that many of the porters and cleaners who work at Goldsmiths can no longer afford to live close to the college is a sign of the times. London's property boom has priced them out and many commute long distances to work from Medway and the hinterlands of Kent or Croydon and the outer rings of the southeast London suburbs where rents are cheaper and property more affordable.

Goldsmiths has attracted much larger numbers of international students, particularly at postgraduate level, and their presence brings a different texture to student life. The academic fortunes of Goldsmiths have burgeoned and the shabby college in a part of London that time forgot has become a 'cool brand'. Through all of these changes, as I hope you will see, something of the mystique of the place – its anarchic, uncontainable and congenial vitality – has persisted.

My intention here is not merely to offer a personal or local story and I hope there is something in these pages that resonates with the experience of other people in higher education both nationally and internationally. While it is a single voice, I want it to be read as a kind of compendium of the things that I have found useful and shared very often through the experience of others.

Ratology

In London you are never more than 12 feet away from a rat, or so the popular legend has it. I don't mean the two-legged variety that can lurk in the corner of an underground carriage or a faculty common room. No, I am thinking narrowly, of quad-footed vermin. At the beginning of the academic year rude evidence of their presence confronted a Goldsmiths student as she strolled through the back streets of south London. A rat had been freshly ironed into the asphalt by a superior creature with four wheels.

The shriek of this first-year student – whom I had just had the pleasure of teaching – drew my attention. I scurried up the street to see the evidence for myself. The vertically challenged beast was a pretty unpleasant sight. The stain on the road gave weight – if not depth – to the urban myth that these monsters are among us at every turn.

A strange sense of responsibility to the new students is strongly felt. Perhaps the dread on their faces reminds me of my own initial encounter with the College as an 18-year-old. Whatever the reason, I feel a strong impulse to do something that pre-empts a repeat. So, off I go to the porter's lodge in search of a plan. 'There's a dead rat in Laurie Grove that's been splattered all over the road.' Mick, the head porter, shrugs his shoulders: 'There's nothin' we can do about it.' 'Well, do you have a shovel?' 'Yeah, there's one 'round the back.' He returns with a tool that has been left, perhaps predictably, by a building contractor who hasn't returned to finish a job. He hands over the large shovel that is coloured with a green patina by what builders call affectionately 'muck'.

It must have been a bizarre spectacle. An hour ago I had been proselytizing from the lectern about the merits of the 'sociological imagination'. And now here I was wandering around the college wielding a large shovel for no apparent reason. I bump into a couple of students from the morning's lecture who look bemused. 'We're building the universities of the future,' I explain and get a cheap laugh in return. This is only half a joke. The realities of packing more students into the same lecture rooms and the financial constraints on higher education are causing a real accommodation crisis. Perhaps a bit of academic self-build is not such a bad idea!

Returning to the crime scene I see that someone has placed a prawn cocktail crisp packet over the cadaver of the ex-rat, maybe out of respect. The shovel is put to work. With cringing application and eyes averted, the task of extra-curricular housekeeping is completed and the rat is entombed in a 'wheelie bin'. Return the shovel and that will be the end of it.

Walking back towards the porter's lodge, I bump into Darren, one of Mick's colleagues. I explain what I'd been doing. 'What did you do that for?' says Darren. 'It took an art student hours to squash that rat . . . I think they call it installation art.' It did cross my mind fleetingly that maybe he was right. If Damien Hirst can bisect a shark, why not squash a rat? Goldsmiths was voted one of Britain's top fifty 'coolest brands'. I am sure this is the result of its celebrity alumni including artist Hirst, comedian Julian Clary, poets and musical figures like Linton Kwesi Johnson and rock band Blur.

This award and the absurdity of the whole 'rat incident' triggered the imagination.

Wasn't a half-eaten mouse mounted on a cappuccino cup lid on this very street last year? Maybe an anonymous art terrorist, with Situationist tendencies, is hidden away in the 'College of Kool'? Perhaps white tape should outline the place where this pesticide victim met its maker? This fable from the beginning of term put a completely different inflection on Walter Benjamin's street walker 'who goes botanising the asphalt'. On my next caffeine-induced wander I should perhaps take a flower for Dear Departed Ratty.

It is the politicians who need flattening, and they might do well to spend a week walking in the footsteps of first-year undergraduates. As Georges Perec said, 'To live is to move from one space to another, while trying as far as possible to avoid bumping into anything'. Perhaps in our time it is also a matter of avoiding stepping on anything unspeakable.

Students Not Suspects

I give a talk at the beginning of term on the challenges and rewards of scholarship to the new intake of graduate research students. It is always a pleasure. The MPhil/PhD students personify the university's future as they gather in induction week – intellect, creativity and restlessness, potential and increasingly cosmopolitanism. Much of what is good about university life is on display in that room year in year out. They enrich institutions but as the UK Higher Education International Unit has pointed out, Britain sells more brainpower per capita than any other country in the world.

In 2009 a Universities UK study entitled 'The impact of universities on the UK economy' found that gross earnings from overseas students in the higher education sector was some £53 billion. While Britain has 1% of the world's population, 5% of the world's scientific research is conducted in the UK and scholars working in British universities produce 14% of the world's most highly cited papers. At the end of the session in 2010 students stay behind to ask about the details of references to follow up or how to find the room the next session is in. A female student waited until all her colleagues had filed out before approaching to ask her question: it wasn't about the content of the lecture. She said she was from China and wanted to talk about her treatment by the UK Border Agency. Her sense of shock was contained in the way she recounted the indignities she was subjected to; there was a stunned look on her face.

'They questioned me about my husband, our marriage – they thought it was fake, as if my whole life was a lie.' I told her she wasn't alone and that it was shameful, a scandal. I also told her that there was a campaign that is trying to do something about the Border Agency's treatment of students and staff.

The 'Students Not Suspects' campaign is a broad coalition of students, academics and activists who are concerned about the impact that shifts in immigration rules are having on international students and the life of the university. Student migration has become heavily politicized in the UK. In September 2010 Damian Green, the Immigration Minister, reported that student visas had risen from 186,000 in 2004 to 307,000 in 2009. He claimed that one in five students remain in Britain after their visa expires and that only half of the students are studying degree courses.

Students have become the latest object of fear and panic within the debate about immigration and global population mobility. In the public debate new phrases such as 'bogus students' (accused of using higher learning illegitimately to gain visas) and 'backstreet colleges' (who are selling immigration and not education) are gaining currency. This is despite the fact that students play an essential role in the economy. Overseas students are in effect subsidizing UK universities and in future this income may become increasingly significant to the financial survival of universities. The Chinese student I spoke to after my lecture is paying three or four times more to study in Britain than her fellow PhD students. In financial terms she is not one student but four. The same study estimated that the personal contribution overseas students make through their off-campus spending was £2.3 billion. In addition, overseas non-university students who have legally extended their visas are working in the health and social care industry where there are labour shortages. There is a paradox at the heart of this debate.

British universities are increasingly globalized or what Bill Readings refers to as 'post-historical'. Readings argues that as a result, the role of today's university has changed profoundly. The university's relationship to the nation-state is no longer what Schiller or Humboldt thought of as a cultural function to foster national tradition and history through the canonization of knowledge. In a globalized world universities become post-historical in the sense that they are no longer preoccupied with the past but with their global rivals in the pursuit of 'excellence' and 'world-class status'. Additionally, UK universities are increasingly seeking new international markets for the recruitment of undergraduate and postgraduate students.

But at the very same time that universities are widening their horizons, the mobility of academics and students is subjected to stricter forms of immigration control. Within the British government's 'points-based immigration system' students from outside the European Economic Area have to prove that they have enough money in their bank account to pay their fees and support themselves. The calculations vary in each case depending on whether the student has 'established' presence (i.e. is already a student) and the location of the university and cost of the course. However, in order to gain maximum points for their case, students have to prove that they have approximately £17,000 in the bank (for both fees and subsistence) for twenty-eight days prior to the receipt of their application.

The lifting of the cap on university fees may further complicate the already Byzantine nature of the process of acquiring a visa. If students are applying from one of forty-two countries listed by the Home Office as posing a specific concern – largely Middle Eastern nations but also including China, Colombia, Brazil and Cuba – then they are expected to register with the police. Students and staff who apply to extend their stay in the UK have to submit biometric information (photograph and fingerprints) and carry an identity card. The result of the points-based system is a sifting and ordering of overseas students into groups who are welcomed for their income and talent and others who are treated with suspicion and prioritized for intense forms of scrutiny.

The British university is being used to further the ends of the nation-state but in a different form. Unlike Bill Readings' image of intellectual and financial flows within the globalized university, higher education is increasingly becoming a pressure point in the politics of border control and migration management. In 2010 the Conservative and Liberal Democrat coalition government established a cap on immigration as a central political pledge. Theresa May, the Home Secretary, has claimed that two-thirds of non-European Union migrants in Britain are students. They number somewhere around 370,000 people.

The university's role is not the German idealist notion of the university as a place to promote national culture, but rather one where border control and the policing of limits of who can belong enter the classroom, including the requirement for university teachers to make their class registers available to the Home Office. This threatens not only to corrode trust between students and teachers but makes university teachers part of the infrastructure of immigration control. This is what the opponents of these measures are resisting and what makes the Students Not Suspects campaign significant. They offer an alternative vision that refuses the creeping erosion of the rights of international students while arguing for a critical understanding of the place of higher education in a world where population mobility is at an unprecedented level.

Students Not Suspects

Anti-immigrant indignation levelled against overseas students is self-defeating in practical economic terms.

Organizations like Migration Watch UK, who applauded the government's crackdown, claim not to be anti-overseas students. Rather, they want 'legitimate students' to study in Britain but insist that they return home afterwards. This ignores the fact that students are not simply 'cash cows'. During these formative years students also fall in love, meet life partners and sometimes have children and imagine their futures here. Many of the greatest minds in Britain – from Nobel Laureates to cultural theorists – have had this experience.

Will students continue to come when experiences like the one I mentioned earlier start to get back – as they surely will – to potential students looking at their options to study abroad? In the context of the cuts in the public financing of universities this threatens to close off the financial potential for universities to balance the shortfall by recruiting abroad. Overseas students, who are bearing the brunt of these measures, will simply take up options elsewhere and take their financial contributions with them. Returning to the room full of young scholars – many of whom are from different parts of the world – the dynamism and energy on display will be damaged if restrictions of student migration result in fewer overseas students in the future. The result will threaten the cosmopolitanism which feeds the exchange of ideas that is the intellectual lifeblood of universities in Britain.

Open Day

On university open day every Vice Chancellor prays for sunshine and a clear blue sky. Even ugly campus architecture or a grim urban location can look appealing bathed in the light of a bright autumn morning. After 2011 open days took on an even greater significance as students measured what they saw against the increased cost of undergraduate study and a £9,000 a year tuition fee. I followed these changes from the 'other side' of the table. My eldest daughter was part of the first undergraduate intake to pay the increased fees. Attending university open days with her was insight into what this looks like from the point of view of our students and their parents.

On a particularly memorable visit to an elite Russell Group university I sat with her in a languages department classroom for an introductory talk about studying modern languages. Some parents were trying to be as inconspicuous as possible, while other parents are armed with burning questions, fists full of highlighter pens and clutching bright manila document wallets packed with QAA (Quality Assurance Agency for Higher Education) teaching scores and research rankings.

Ten minutes after the talk is scheduled to start the admissions tutor walks in. He is carrying an armful of prospectuses and what looks like a bucket-sized cup of coffee. 'I am truly sorry everyone, I got delayed by enquiries at our stall on campus – it's a bit of a One Man Show today. If you could bear with me, I just need to set up the PowerPoint.' The portly linguist then takes another five minutes to load his presentation. With a blink of the projector his first slide appears on screen. We are treated to a truly tortuous introductory talk lasting twenty minutes.

'I am so sorry some of the option courses listed on this slide are no longer available.' Trying to gloss over another error, he says: 'Agh . . . well those admissions figures are actually out of date now . . . but I can email you the latest figures if you would like me to.' An earnest parent asks a question about a particular joint honours degree. He replies: 'Actually, I don't know whether that joint degree programme will be running next year.' In a stumbling finale he confesses: 'Perhaps I should have checked the PowerPoint before giving this talk.' It was a sobering and salutary experience that was very much in mind as I prepared a 'taster lecture in Sociology' for the Goldsmiths October Open Day just a few weeks later.

On that Saturday morning we were blessed with great weather, almost too good. Conditions perfect for sitting in a deck chair rather than a lecture hall. A half an hour prior to my spot I checked the lecture room, loaded the PowerPoint presentation before anyone arrived and left my cup of coffee in the canteen! Fifteen minutes before the scheduled time of the talk prospective students started to file in along with some parents. I had time to kill so I asked a budding sociologist if she had been having a good day. She smiled and said, 'Much better than the other places I've been to!' Listing a series of our prestigious rivals she said she was surprised by how little effort they had put into their Open Days. It seemed to her to reveal something of the smugness of those institutions.

'Top universities' know they will be oversubscribed because

at this point the government had limited the number of places as a consequence of the cost of the student loans scheme.
The result is the institutions she listed don't have to try so hard.
After reflecting on what she said, I replied: 'One of the few
good things that has resulted from all the changes imposed by
the government is that we are having to prioritize the student
experience and value teaching more than we did in the past.'
For institutions in what is being referred to as the 'squeezed
middle' our future depends on giving students a better value
experience. I heard myself say, 'Perhaps, that is why there is so
much at stake for us and why days like today matter.'

Looking up I noticed that the parents in the tiered
seats were hanging on every word of the conversation.
Perhaps for some of them the 'brand value' of a degree will start
to matter less than what students experience in the classroom.
At dinner that night I asked my daughter what she had learned
from the numerous university open days she had attended.
She replied: 'Well, your whole impression of a university can
be transformed by just one good experience.' It focuses the
mind to think that every member of faculty and staff has that
gift within their power on Open Day.

Stuart Hall Lessons

Listening to Stuart Hall made us see the world differently and he had a gift that enabled us to understand our life anew. He seemed to be talking directly to you, even if it was through the TV screen or through the pages of one of his many influential essays. I think that is why so many people – even students and readers who never met him in person – felt such a deep sense of personal loss at the news of his passing on 10 February 2014. It was as if a bright star that gave us a bearing in life to navigate our course had fallen from the sky.

In the sixties and seventies he helped define the New Left as a political movement that broke free of the intellectual confinements of Cold War thinking. Along with Richard Hoggart, he established the Centre for Contemporary Cultural Studies at Birmingham that offered a completely radical way to understand the unfolding drama of British social life as its economic power withered and the 'workshop of the world' was reduced to industrial ruins. It is not without irony that it took someone like Stuart Hall – a Rhodes scholarship boy from Jamaica – to develop a clear-sighted view of what British culture was becoming as the sun set on its empire. He was also the first intellectual to comprehend the deep impact that the authoritarian populism of Conservative Prime Minister Margaret Thatcher would have on shaping Britain's post-imperial future.

For him thinking was always a process of transformation and changing himself, making sense out of the senselessness of exploitation, imperialism and racism. If you followed his thought you could not help but be transformed too. It was impossible ever to drink a cup of tea again without being reminded of the imperial traces in the brown leaves and the sugar's sweet taste. Stuart Hall was interested in what you had to say and in conversation he would use phases such as 'of course you have written about that'. The sense of acknowledgement was incredibly validating, conveying a sense that you were playing a part in a much bigger project of transformation.

He rarely got embroiled in personal infighting within the anti-racist Left and I think he had a sense of where deep defining political fault lines lay in the struggle for a more just society. He helped you keep your mind open and to resist what Freud called the 'narcissism of minor differences'. It is a terrible prospect to contemplate the world without his wisdom and counsel. The weekend before he died I was reading one of his lesser known essays, 'Marx's Notes on Method: A Reading of the "1857 Introduction"', that was published in a CCCS collection. Reading his words on the page I could almost hear his unique voice, his sense of humour and his joy in understanding something important as if for the first time. These are precious gifts bequeathed to us in his writing.

Stuart Hall had an incredible capacity for intellectual generosity. He could unlock a student trapped by an intellectual conundrum with a single phrase. I witnessed this first hand in relation to a student he encountered at Goldsmiths. I wrote to Stuart afterwards to let him know the impact of that one chance meeting and the letter I think captures something profound about his special qualities as a teacher and radical pedagogue:

Stuart Hall Lessons

28 July 2000

Dear Stuart Hall,

Re: Small kindnesses that count

I have been meaning to write this letter for a couple of months, sadly the distraction of exam boards and academic bureaucracy got in the way. That is until now. I have followed and admired your work and thinking for a long time and the fingerprints of your influences are all over my own flawed attempts. But I am not writing to acknowledge and thank you for those gifts (though, thanks are certainly deserved).

Some months ago you came to Goldsmiths to Angela McRobbie's inaugural lecture. That night you met one of my students called Mónica. I hope you remember her. Mónica is from Mexico and she has been working through the issues of race and identity that are central to her own biography. In our talks she would say that she felt 'caught in between' in the vice-like grip of 'mixed race' ontology. Her mother is 'white' and her father 'black'. I tried to tell her – parroting cultural theory – that this was not a problem of her making, but an effect of the way race and identity is understood. As much as I tried to offer a way out of the vice, the tighter it seemed to grip her in her everyday life.

The day after Angela's lecture Mónica knocked on my door. She came in and sat down. We started to talk. She told me that she'd met you and that with her friend Meeta you'd talked about a whole range of things. As she told me about your conversation it seemed as if a whole burden had been lifted from her. She said that she had repeated to you the things that she had said to me so many, many times. Then she recounted that you told her that 'people like you are the people of the future'. This one phrase did what countless tutorials and hours of erudition had failed to achieve. Something clicked. She'd escaped the grip of thinking 'in-between' as a confinement. It is something of a wonder to me that such a small thing – a few words of kind insight – has affected so much change in one person.

Mónica has moved on. She's developing her own critique of 'race thinking' and her own ideas about the strengths and limits in the work of the people she admires the most. She plans to do a PhD on race thinking in Mexico. It's been really something to witness. Makes me understand that small moments like this have more political efficacy than a thousand pages of well meant words of 'keyboard radicalism'.

I hope this letter finds you well. I really enjoyed listening to your 'Desert Island Discs' and I hope to have an opportunity to talk to you about your love of Miles Davis at some point (I have been mass producing my recording of the programme and sending it to friends around the world). I am also enclosing a range of things that have emerged from the Centre for Urban and Community Research here at Goldsmiths. I have been involved in CUCR since 1994 and we've been trying to connect theory and practice in our work in a way that tries to address a wider popular and policy audience. I've also enclosed some of our working papers.

Sincere thanks and best wishes,

Les Back

Mónica Moreno Figueroa completed her PhD with distinction and she has taught at Newcastle University and now lectures in Sociology at Cambridge. After Stuart died I wrote to Mónica and asked her about her memories of that time. I will add her own reflections shortly. There is something urgent we need to remember as we pay tribute to Stuart and his generous intellect. Before returning to them, I want to mention how Mónica – now an established teacher and academic – remembered that far off time and her own memories triggered by the sad news of Stuart's passing.

> *When learning about Stuart Hall's death and then going through the rush of countless emails, Facebook posts and newspaper articles, a raw sense of mourning took over me, reading and feeling through the enormity of such a great life. Many have told amazing stories about their encounters with him, his words, thoughts and interventions. The first time they read his work, the many occasions they listened to one of his eye-opening lectures, the last time they spoke to him, the longstanding inspiration, the tremendous contribution to critical thinking and, amongst it all, the opportunities and encouragement he extended to so many, especially the ones commonly excluded, usually invisible. Like others, I was compelled to hold onto memories, phrases, ideas, just to say something as a way of grasping the loss of someone truly remarkable. I too unearthed this letter that Les Back had so generously written to Stuart Hall and copied to me. I have kept it preciously.*
>
> *When I came to Goldsmiths from Mexico to do an MA, I had no understanding of theoretical discussions about race, nor any grasp of how to start voicing what the experience of racism felt like. Goldsmiths threw me into a kind of rough sea that challenged what I knew, both academically and personally. That context and the very brief encounter I had with Stuart Hall, with his undivided attention to a story which surely he had heard many times, was wonderfully significant, allowing me to think about the politics of injustice, the need to turn questions upside down, and to move from shame and perplexity to reflexive anger and compassion. He allowed me to make of something I thought personal, a life's task.*
>
> *Just a couple of weeks ago, I was discussing Stuart Hall's 'The West and The Rest: Discourse and Power' with students at Newcastle University, focusing on the trajectory and impact of*

constructions of difference and value for understanding notions of race. His insights enable us to put contexts such as Mexico and Britain into productive conversation. He offers us ways of connecting the apparently disjointed, of thinking in terms of the big picture at the same time as the ordinary and the unremark-able. Les Back's question, 'what would Stuart Hall do?' is key, as an invitation for daring and creative ways of thinking, gen-erous approaches to learning and sharing, and to pursue clear political ways to intervene in the world.

Mónica Moreno Figueroa

Stuart Hall's life offers us an alternative path to follow in the vocation of thinking and learning. It is fitting that in late 2014 the building where Goldsmiths' Media and Communications department is housed was renamed The Professor Stuart Hall Building in his memory. Stuart was committed to intervening publically in the key political questions. He never followed a narrow academic path but knew theory was an essential lens for critique. We should honour that by asking, at any given point in a political argument or in an encounter with a student: 'what would Stuart Hall do?' Then, having established an an-swer with our own wits, act accordingly.

Teaching

Academics should see themselves first as teachers. In my view any faculty member working in a university who doesn't like teaching or goes to every effort to minimize their contact with students should really consider doing something else. Students are our first public and often our most important audience and some of them are also our future colleagues. There is something deeply troubling in the extent to which the priorities of university life – despite the rhetoric of teaching quality and research-led teaching – make teaching an activity of secondary importance.

There is no doubt that the commodification of higher learning has transformed the student experience. They not only have to save up and pay for studying but as a consequence students more and more see themselves as consumers. 'I needed to get a 2.1 in your class,' complains the student on receiving his grade of 52. The complaint is not simply connected to an unfulfilled aspiration but he feels he is owed a return on the cold hard cash he has paid in student fees. Regardless of these changes and all the things that go can wrong in the classroom there are still those precious moments. It doesn't happen all the time but it is when the teacher, in that moment, has somehow caught the imagination of the whole group. You can feel a dense silence that hangs over the room almost as if everyone in the lecture hall has stopped breathing. It is hard to put a price tag on that deep attentive silence and it is why teaching still matters.

On 22 April 2008 the University of Warwick's innovative Reinvention Centre for Undergraduate Research hosted an exhibition created by Cath Lambert and Elisabeth Simbuerger called 'Teaching and Learning in and for a Complex World'. It aimed to open up a dialogue around teaching and scholarship. Attending the launch at The Teaching Grid in Warwick's central library I was struck by how the sentiments that adorned its smooth glass surfaces seemed out of step with the priorities of the twenty-first-century British university. Along the glass walls leading into the exhibition a quotation from Joseph Beuys in bold letters proclaimed: 'To be a teacher is my greatest work of art.'

A sound installation called 'Sociologists Talking' formed a key part of the exhibition, drawn from interviews conducted by Elisabeth Simbuerger with sociologists about their work, teaching and aspirations. The installation offered an opportunity to eavesdrop on the conversations that we are all having with our colleagues, friends and even ourselves about the state of the academy. Each set of headphones was connected to a digital voice recorder with twenty minutes of talk looped continuously. Actors reconstructed the voices in order to protect the anonymity of the participants and the interview transcripts were performed as in a play. All the 'informants'/'characters' were drawn from a single department in a university from the Russell Group. Only Elisabeth was identifiable; she played herself.

Regardless of the priority given to research and publishing, most of those recorded said that teaching gave them a sense of intellectual purpose. Sociology here is valued for its ability to question that which is assumed and normalized. Teaching offers a kind of intellectual sociability which, in the words of one contributor, 'militates against the isolation . . . which is quite inherent to [the] academic work of research'. The impetus so often is to encourage a search for research funds that enables being 'bought out of teaching' in order to dedicate time to research and writing. Like most interview data, Simbuerger's might be best interpreted as a moral tale, a reflection of the speaker's principles rather than a description of their daily choices and routines. Regardless, such a sentiment reveals the first paradox: the educational ethos may value teaching highly but academic success necessitates a quest to minimize the amount of time spent in the classroom.

Another set of voice recordings within the exhibition was entitled 'Teaching for Complexity'. This sequence of quotations concerned the issue of what university education is needed for in our time. The task, the interviewees suggested, is to engender an 'enthusiasm for learning' but also to encourage students to lead what one respondent called 'an examinant life'.

Education, the voices suggested, is not simply an invitation to engage with life differently, but also an invitation to reside in books and dwell within the abstract landscape of theoretical ideas.

> I mean, 'How do you learn to live in a text?' is like saying 'How do you learn to live in a new city?' How do you learn to live there? Well, when you first live there your knowledge of it is very superficial, yeah. There are all sorts of things in it that you don't know and that you are therefore not receptive to or appreciative of.

This analogy was developed further. Like an unfamiliar city, theoretical ideas can be initially confusing and disorientating.

Students need to get lost in order to find something of value and this takes time, effort and commitment. The relationship to theoretical reading is summed up beautifully by one contributor as 'the difference between getting information out of a text and living in it'.

Yet, the pressure placed on students to do paid work throughout their university education undermines such a level of engagement with ideas. Students are not going to find paid employment living in the city of books. Many of our educational ideals were defined in an era before student fees and loans, when many of us who are now members of the sociological professoriate – myself included – benefited from free university education. This difference is communicated powerfully in the film *Students at Work* produced as part of the exhibition.

In a time when education is a commodity, little wonder that students are goal-oriented and have an instrumental view of education. Therein lies another paradox: some of our most dearly held educational values are in direct conflict with the economic and practical conditions within which teaching takes place. As a result, the pressure and temptation to simplify the curriculum and make courses less demanding and more 'student friendly' militates against the commitment to spend time with difficult ideas.

The sentiments articulated in this installation sum up the fraught nature of the choices and accommodations that we face. A contributor set out the choice in the following stark terms:

> I think most people at a university like this recognize that if you want to get a career, if you want to advance, if you want promotion, it doesn't matter how good or innovative a teacher you are, it counts for nothing really. You're much better getting publications, a reputation at conferences, PhD students, than you are getting a reputation as a great teacher of undergraduates, that's my view.

Teaching

The quantitative measurement of academic value and performance are a part of the increased marketization of the sector. The auditing of research undercuts the place of teaching within an academic vocation, fostering instead a disciplined careerism that is both self-involved and by implication ridden with anxiety.

> That quantitative measure has meant in effect that most of us have been pushed into a position of either saying 'I don't care about a career, I'm really interested in teaching students,' or you have to say 'If I care about a career I've got to publish stuff.' And to publish in our present conditions of work means neglecting other things, and unfortunately teaching is one of the easiest to neglect, because there aren't really any direct forms of accountability.

The impact of universities being dependent on increased student fees for their income is adding another dimension to this situation. Marina Warner's tale of why in 2014 she quit her job as Professor in the Department of Literature, Film and Theatre Studies at the University of Essex after ten years indicates another twist. Under pressure from Essex Vice Chancellor Anthony Foster – who has a military background – faculty were pressed to turn their priorities away from research and publication and the Research Excellent Framework towards teaching and increased student recruitment as a way of generating more income. Sounding like a character from Frank Parkin's campus satire *The Mind and Body Shop*, Foster put his dismay bluntly when he said at a public meeting: 'These REF stars – they don't earn their keep.' This way of prioritizing teaching is little more than a commercial imperative with nothing to do with the ethics of learning and teaching. Evidently all appeals to value teaching are not necessarily good for life of the mind.

Neither is it the case that all pleas to value research have a progressive impact on knowledge. The injunction to produce more research doesn't necessarily result in more communication. Perhaps the ultimate indictment contained here is that the profusion of sociological literature that results from making research the ultimate priority finds limited if any readership.

> People write books and nobody reads them, thousands of journals that nobody reads. However, students are real people, and they come and they are expecting some degree of quality in what they get at university. And I have to say, many people who are employed as university teachers, in my view, don't give that quality. They regard teaching as something secondary to the great adventure of discovering new knowledge that no one is interested in.

Academic writing in this characterization is little more than a language game, prestige without value, knowledge that does little to nourish the imagination or even command attention. Such a characterization is resonant of Lindsay Waters' damning critique of academic publishing in America. As an executive editor for Harvard University Press, Waters has monitored shifts in academic life from inside the belly of the beast. The result, he argues, is the overproduction of 'unread' and 'unloved' books. He suggests academic books are not written now to be read or loved, rather they are written to be counted. The concern to communicate ideas is trumped by the requirement to get jobs, secure tenure and establish a reputation. Academic overproduction means that reputations are made in fleeting assessments, not judged through careful erudition but based on speed-reading or second-hand judgements – 'I have a friend who read that book and they hated it!' Certain judgements made with minimal knowledge.

Let me sum up: at least three paradoxes could be heard in the voices of Simbuerger's university teachers. First, while

Teaching

teaching is valued as a connection to what Michael Burawoy refers to as our first public (i.e. students), academic success necessitates keeping that contact to a minimum. Second, our most dearly held education values – such as the importance of 'living in books' and exploring difficult ideas – are proving harder to sustain in the face of the priorities that take time away from learning and teaching. Third, the injunction to write more academically leads to less academic writing actually being read. Are these open secrets? If they are then no wonder that the dominant atmosphere in universities is timidity and quietism. Perhaps we can't quite believe, or accept, what we have become. Teaching remains an antidote in my view because it offers those precious heavy silences where we are thinking together and when everyone is holding their breath.

The Uses of Literacy Today

It was a real honour today to be asked to speak at the event *Celebrating the Life and Work of Richard Hoggart*, not least because Richard Hoggart – who died in 2014 – was the Warden of the college when I was a student here in the 1980s. It was something of a comfort then – in the midst of the vertigo of a non-traditional student's experience of university life – to know that someone like Richard Hoggart was in charge. Regardless of his lofty title, Hoggart had grown up as a young man in a working-class world in Hunslet, Yorkshire. He had in part been drawn to Goldsmiths because of its association with the arts and humanities but also because of the college's commitment to offering adult education locally.

In 1989 Hoggart wrote an introduction to a then new edition of George Orwell's *The Road to Wigan Pier*. He commented that in 1937, when Orwell's book was published, it was fashionable to say that class divisions were fading. Then twenty years later when he published *The Uses of Literacy* the same kinds of things were being said in the year that Harold Macmillan said boldly, 'Many of our people have never had it so good.'

Hoggart wrote, 'Class distinctions do not die, they merely learn new ways of expressing themselves . . . Each decade we swiftly declare we have buried class; each decade the coffin stays empty.'

I think the question that remains an open one is how to best understand and write about the vitality of class as it is lived and felt. What *The Uses of Literacy* offers us is some answers to that question that are beyond time and place. Many people have a sense that their own lives or the people that they know and love are written into this book in some way. It provided luminous fragments of classed feeling and sensation. It comes through in the ways he writes about food, the cheap cuts like pig's feet and liver, but also his descriptions of occasional luxuries of tinned pineapple or tinned red salmon that is, as he puts it, 'far tastier than fresh salmon'. It is a specific observation that is resonant with a wider feeling even when the specific details vary.

Hoggart's account of the northern cities of his childhood is often misrepresented as sentimental. Writing about the same charge levelled against Orwell, he comments: 'That final "-al" in "sentimental" is an escape mechanism – to escape from considering the true expression of "sentiment".' So much of the richness of class sentiment escapes or slips out of the ways in which we write about the sociology of class today.

Hoggart himself is scathing of the images of working-class people made from simply 'adding together the variety of statistics given in some of the sociological works'. He might have been writing about the thin descriptions contained in the recent BBC Great British Class Survey. *The Uses of Literacy* is written with a sometimes shuddering and withering honesty. Much is made of his use of autobiography but I actually read him as a kind of proto-ethnographer of not just his own life, but the life of the world he remained part of well into his thirties, however tenuously.

Hoggart's female characters are the real heroines of this book. I would argue, along with people like Sue Owen, that there is something distinguishing about Hoggart's account of the lives of working-class women. While the overall frame of

54

the book remains patriarchal, the women are extraordinary. Consider this passage:

> She had the spirits, and I say this with no intention of disparaging her, of a mongrel bitch. She fought hard and constantly for her children, but it never 'got 'er down', though she often exploded with temper among them. She was without subservience or deference, or a desire to win pity.

Women like that are recognizable today but their struggle is against the new moralism of class hatred that is of a different order of governmental structure and control.

What would those vital fragments of class feeling include now? They'd include the nail salon, the sun bed, the tattoos of children and relatives that are inscribed on adult working-class bodies like kinship diagrams and the Technicolor excess of the Christmas lights that decorate working-class homes.

I think much critical attention has focused on what Hoggart saw as the 'spiritual dry-rot' of the world of rock'n'roll and milk bars and the threat of a historic break. There is also something else that he outlines about the ways in which the 'older attitudes' carried through time. It's captured in the phrase about middle-aged folk: 'Agh, you sound more like your mother every day.' It makes me think how limited our understanding of these feelings is within the council estates of our cities.

I have been going to a lot of funerals of men and women who came of age in Hoggart's 'candyfloss' world. I am struck by how much the elemental structures of classed feeling – the personal, concrete and the local – endure through time. It is somehow captured and brought back to life in those funereal eulogies.

My last point is about what is not in this extraordinary book. In July 1939 George Orwell wrote in the pages of *Adelphi* magazine that 'what we always forget is that the overwhelming bulk of the British proletariat does not live in Britain, but in Asia and

Africa'. It is a warning against the ways class culture is still colonized by a normalizing sense of whiteness. Today more of the
British proletariat – in the way Orwell would define it – lives
in Britain, but their experience is not confined to these islands.

This summer I went to the appropriately named Home Park
in Sydenham to hear Janet Kay and Carol Thompson perform
their Lover's Rock anthems. Lover's Rock is a sweet form of
melodic reggae music that was pioneered in London in the
late 1970s and 1980s through innovators like Dennis Bovell
but featuring lots of local people. When Janet Kay sang 'Silly
Games' the crowd of all shades and three generations erupted.
It made me think of Hoggart's club singers and the songs that
he characterizes as expressing the 'feeling heart'. The song animated shared sentiments across the line of colour within what
seemed to me a profoundly classed experience. They'd gone to
the same schools, lived in the same areas and had to contend,
perhaps in varying degrees, with the same social workers and
defenders of law and moral order.

It seems really vital – remembering Stuart Hall's observation
– to think about how race and ethnicities serve as the modali-
ties through which class is lived, as well as how class is the mo-
dality through which race is lived. In order to do this we need
a much better understanding of culture as a structure of feeling
that contains traditional elements with emergent forms, that is
made in place but where the here and elsewhere of history and
culture is part of that interaction.

While Hoggart was personally liberal and open-minded on
issues of race, he was less sanguine about the forms of anti-racist politics that emerged in the early 1980s, particularly in response to the 1981 New Cross Fire when thirteen black teenag-
ers lost their lives just a street away. He was sceptical of the link
between the fire and accusations of racism levelled against the
police for their failure to prosecute those responsible.

The striking thing when remembering Richard Hoggart is
his lifelong commitment to education. It came through in the

democratic clarity of his books and the intelligent sense of purpose of his arguments. It's not just that working-class readers recognized themselves in his books but he inspired them to be more than the 'persuaders of modern life' offered. Hoggart was an inspiring and dedicated teacher, a legacy of his days as an extra-mural teacher at Hull in the late forties.

Even as Warden of Goldsmiths he continued to teach, contributing lectures on his literary heroes such as D.H. Lawrence and W.H. Auden. The value of education for Hoggart was in thinking together critically in an open and inclusive way. The task of the university was, as he put it, 'to intellectualize its neighbourhood'. Isobel Armstrong – his first PhD student – commented, 'Teaching was at the centre of his life.'

There is a scene in his memoir *An Imagined Life* that illustrates his commitment to teaching. During the seventies and eighties academic staff at Goldsmiths had to apply to Senate House to become a 'Recognised Teacher of the University'. This indignity was the result of Goldsmiths not being a full and equal member of the University of London. It was a kind of academic quality check. As an active teacher, Hoggart mischievously made an application; he thought 'so long as it exists' he should 'go through the same hoops' even though he was the head of the college. This caused the university bureaucrats at Senate House considerable embarrassment because it made the second-class status of Goldsmiths academics cringingly evident.

In his memoir he describes a student that embodied 'Goldsmiths' peculiar strengths'. A young woman of about thirty, she had escaped a series of dead-end jobs and been given a grant by the Local Educational Authority to study English at Goldsmiths. Richard Hoggart – the Warden of the College – was her seminar teacher. After a seminar he asked her how she was getting on. She said she was finding the commuting from north London, and also the disciplined routine of study, difficult. 'But,' she added, 'it's wonderful. I can't get over the fact that I'm being *paid* to read books all day.' Sadly, the same luxurious opportunity offered to this student is not available – except to a limited few – today. Now students have to *pay* to read books all day. This politically manufactured indebtedness is a betrayal of a whole generation but it is also a betrayal of Hoggart's vision of education's power and value.

As Stefan Collini rightly pointed out, this is more than just a matter of the introduction of student fees. Rather, it is about the full marketization of higher education and introduction of new commercial players into the once publically funded educational sector. The political intent is to split higher education into an elite of selective universities and 'a selection of cheap degree shops offering cut-price value for money'. Collini argues in the new candyfloss world of higher education once first-rate universities are turned into third-rate businesses.

As they find themselves in a new situation something eats away at faculty, as metrics are used to measure and judge their academic worth. 'It is the alienation from oneself that is experienced by those who are forced to describe their activities in misleading terms,' Collini concluded. This is reminiscent of Coleridge, who put it rather well when he wrote that the value of a person is 'to be weighed not counted'.

So many of us are Hoggart's children. Remembering him now I realize how much his life and work provided an outline for my own. Among the ruins of the university of commerce are the embers of what Hoggart called the 'Great Tradition' of transformative learning. This is best captured in Albert Mansbridge's idea that adult education is a 'collective highway'. For Hoggart this was the refusal to accept intellectual wantlessness, where thinking can suture and balm lives that feel as if they are falling apart, where we have the right to ask to be more than what we already are. As teachers in his wake, we are left with the difficult task of ensuring that those embers do not go cold.

Death by PowerPoint

The style of academic performance has undergone a quiet makeover. The clumsy rustling of notes set against the backdrop of a broken overhead projector or upside down slideshow has been replaced by the slick digital wizardry of PowerPoint and 'data projection'. This transformation is worthy of a reality TV miracle. Busily hooking up my laptop at a recent conference in Copenhagen, a friend who had been working abroad asked: 'Does everyone do that now? All looks very corporate!' The edge in his aside made me realize quite how fast and completely things have changed.

The increasingly digitized forms of academic performance have a downside. The worst example I've witnessed was a conference in America where a sociologist merely read the content of his talk from the large shimmering screen. During the entire paper he had his back turned to the audience. This was not a knowing academic version of Bob Dylan's famous stage antics. It was as if he was speaking to his new gadget or worshipping it as if it were an altar of ideas.

The 'bullet point effect' can produce a situation where presentations seem like a long series of lists without much exposition. Complex argument cannot be crafted through a series of quick-fire points at the click of a mouse. Here technological sophistication results paradoxically in less textured communication. Presentations that suffer from this syndrome can result in something akin to a nail-gun approach to thinking. Like all technological innovations though, this is a matter of how it is used and not the technology itself. While there might be risks in relying on these technologies, there are also real opportunities.

A study of PowerPoint usage by educationalist Stephen Dobson, published in 2006, claimed the real prospect offered by this technology is that academics can display and evoke ideas in new ways and 'exhibit themselves' differently. Using what Walter Benjamin called the 'mimetic faculty', Dobson argues that the challenge is to communicate and make 'connections between different senses and to assign meaning to these connections'. Such a multi-modal (textual, imagist and spoken) approach might just be the most useful way of approaching the technology. Here the interplay between vision, text and sound may help evoke ideas and reflection.

This is something I've been trying to experiment with in my own teaching. At the end of one of my courses last year a student said after completing the quantitative course review form: 'I really like your lectures and the way you use music, sound and pictures – it kind of leaves a trace on all your senses that makes you think again afterwards.' It was the best compliment about my teaching I've ever been paid. PowerPoint offers more options to blend words, sound and vision and it is for this reason that it offers a major resource.

Too often though, I think conference presentations are less about the 'exhibition of ideas' and more about the display of academic credentials and distinction. For a properly turned out academic to be taken seriously it seems three things are needed: a research centre logo to brand their PowerPoint presentation, a web address and, increasingly, being smartly dressed in a good costume. Perhaps this version of academic performance is not unrelated to the pressure all of us feel to undergo an impression management drive in anticipation of the next audit of 'research excellence'. However, reliance on PowerPoint, or for that matter any other form of multimedia, means that professional undoing and embarrassment can be just a click of the mouse away.

At the public lecture mentioned earlier I lined up a full array of PowerPoint gimmicks with the assistance of my laptop, including photographs, sound clips, animation and text. At the end of the talk questions followed from the audience, but while I was doing my best to answer them something quite unplanned unfolded behind me. I take the laptop home and my children make use of it for their homework and also their weakness for social media. Unknown to me Stevie, 12 years old at the time, had set the screensaver function to a 'My Pictures Slideshow'. As I talked earnestly about the 'war on terror' and the London bombings the automatic slideshow treated the audience to a hi-resolution sequence of holiday snaps of my family in various states of beach undress and my kids head-banging with guitars like extras from Jack Black's movie *School of Rock*.

Completely unaware, I continued to pronounce on Samuel Huntingdon's 'clash of civilizations' thesis and London's multicultural landscape. No one said a word until a young Dane approached me afterwards. In a strange Scandinavian variant of a mid-Atlantic drawl he said, 'Nice slideshow and nice guitars. Is that Les Paul Gold Top yours?' Realizing that a secret self had inadvertently been revealed, I replied, 'Er yes, it is.' Doing my best to make small talk through the embarrassment I feared that I had unwittingly become a character in a scene from a yet to be written David Lodge novel. Not very flattering and in the end not very corporate! The lesson is perhaps to be wary of the computer's uncanny potential and always check your screensaver setting.

The Value in Academic Writing

Some writers' names become associated with whole ways of knowing. Their designation makes the conversion from an individual noun to a system of thought, even if that system is not always very systematic. 'This is why,' writes Clifford Geertz, 'we tend to discard their first names after a while and adjectvise their last ones' – Foucauldian, Freudian, Marxist, Kleinian and so on. Really big names are transmuted to eponyms. They become what Barthes referred to as 'author priests'. By contrast the rest of us academic artisans are little more than clerks or at best apostles. The implication is that academic authors fall into either the rare breed of intellectual giants or mere typists transcribing the obscure trivialities of life and translating them into terms that are already set.

The cumulative effect is that attempts to write seem doomed or compromised to merely adding a few footnotes when compared to the high priests of theory. In Britain, academics are judged on a geographical scale of acclaim: to write 'world class' publications is the ultimate aspiration and the very least an academic should possess is a 'national profile'. The audits, whether the Research Assessment Exercise or the Research Excellence Framework, aim to rank departments and distribute funds . . . excellently.

The consequences have been profoundly damaging both to thought and academic literature. Timidity, conservatism and hyper-specialization reign. It comes through in the way academics speak of their expertise: 'I couldn't form an opinion because it is outside my area.' That subject area might be a mile deep as Paul Gilroy has commented, but it is only an inch wide. We have become inured to this absurd and obscene system that measures and ranks intellectual value in a crass equivalent of a 'hit parade' of books and journal articles. Could any scholar go along her/his bookshelves and rank numerically the works of great philosophers and visionary thinkers in this way? What grade would Gramsci's *Prison Notebooks* receive as compared to Arendt's *Life of the Mind*? Who would be number one? It would be incongruous even to try and the effort would cheapen us intellectually as this pernicious system has the whole UK university sector. Indeed, the victories produced through the Research Assessment Exercise are as hollow as the defeats.

Regardless of the injunction to assess and measure, the process of auditing intellectual value is always partisan and fated to guesswork. It is like trying to weigh handfuls of water against each other as the liquid slips through the fingers. Can we even know the value of our own work? I think not and moreover it is a mistake even to try to measure it. There are rare moments when that elusive worth is revealed. It is certainly not when the deliberations of the research assessment panels are announced.

A few years ago I gave a lecture in Dublin. I had finished a new book and embarked on a series of talks to tell people about it in the hope that it might stand an outside chance of being read. To my surprise at the end of the lecture a dozen or so people stayed behind to get their copies signed.

One woman waited until all the others had left. She approached very timidly and then said, 'I really enjoyed your lecture but I just wanted to say "thank you".' I looked back a little confused and said that it was nothing and that I'd really appreciated the questions people had asked. She shook her head – she wasn't referring to this evening. 'I read one of your essays when I was really stuck with my own work. I just couldn't find a way to get beyond this sense of being stuck. Then someone recommended your work and it somehow helped me find a way out and a way to move on.'

She told me about her ethnographic study of young working-class boys' experience of schooling in a part of Dublin inspired by Paul Willis' classic *Learning to Labour*. There was such sincerity in her voice, something that cannot be simulated for effect or advantage. It wasn't a networking opportunity, I never knew her name and we never met again and she never told me which piece of my writing had been of help. Her sense of being stuck was as much about the discomforts of authorship as it was with the technical challenges of written argument. 'I felt like, who was I to say anything? Your essay – which was about your own biography and work – just helped me carry on, helped me finish.'

More than any other measure the value of what writers do, even academic ones, is to provide companionship for further thought. Writing here is less an achievement that is measured extrinsically than an invitation to imagine beyond its own terms of reference. Books and essays here befriend and encourage thinking with interlocutors that remain – except on rare occasions like this one – anonymous. This value cannot be audited or cheapened through the mechanisms that aim to judge, measure and distribute repute and ultimately money.

Research Expenses

What do you need to do a piece of research? In the physical and medical sciences young researchers often need to raise money for expensive technical hardware to enable them just to get started. Laboratory research is expensive. In the humanities it is somewhat different. For the last few years I have served on a University of London small research grants awards committee dedicated to postgraduate students and early career researchers called the Central Research Fund. Up until the abolition of this committee I acted as its chair.

The committee was composed of economists, psychologists, geographers, anthropologists, lawyers and specialists in international relations. The relatively small amounts of money awarded – never more than £2,000 – made an enormous difference to the successful applicants, many of whom were self-funding their doctorates. Each proposal would be evaluated carefully and feedback would often be given to weak applications. The academics gave their time voluntarily. The supportive but vigilantly critical assessments embodied a model of the best values in academic peer-review.

Sometimes the committee would look dimly on inflated budgets or cheeky requests. Luxury items would be ruled out as fanciful, expensive moleskin notebooks dismissed in favour of budget reporter notepads; or exception would be taken to their fund being used to acquire the latest 'high spec' laptop computer. The committee's ethos was both generous and frugal. Each year there would be a handful of requests that would make us smile or even laugh out loud, like the young anthropologist who requested financial support to purchase a camel under the travel section of her budget. Or the student of Stalin's agrarian reforms who requested £130 for half a ton of coal to enable him to heat his room and cook as he travelled through the villages of the former Soviet Union.

The requests would also reveal ethical differences between the academic disciplines represented around the table. It is entirely normal for psychologists to pay informants to participate in their experiments. Others felt that this was questionable ethically. In one case an applicant asked for £56.30 for sweets and gift bags for interviewees as a 'culturally appropriate' form of remuneration. The request raised eyebrows, particularly from the lawyers and political scientists and indeed sociologists like myself.

The process could also reveal some of the different virtues held by academic disciplines. For example, anthropologists would sometimes question requests to pay for translators or research assistants. In anthropology, learning the language and customs of a society through intensive fieldwork is a professional virtue to guard against ethnocentrism and intellectual superficiality.

Each meeting provided a rare realization of interdisciplinary judgement. The university decided to abolish the Central Research Fund in 2009. To their minds it was too inefficient and time intensive. This was regardless of the fact that members gave themselves to the task willingly and objected bitterly to it being shut down. Their work made a difference to countless numbers of students, some of whom subsequently ended up serving on the committee as assessors of the next generation of researchers. The time the committee gave helped the students make the best of their efforts and, more than that, to develop intellectually.

Howard Becker has pointed out that humanities research is actually a relatively low cost affair. 'The materials for recording, storing and analysing interviews and field notes are cheap. Qualitative researchers need money to pay for their time . . .' It takes time to chase leads, talk to people, write field notes, reflect on what's been witnessed, check sources and ultimately to write down what we've learned. Research also involves others not directly involved giving time to the project. In addition to the CRF expert panellists who lent intelligent eyes and ears to the applications, researchers rely on reviewers, supervisors and friends to point to what they cannot see or hear that might well be right in front of them. You cannot budget for this essential resource but without it the task of scholarship is impossible.

Extra Curricular

Academics are not always very likeable. This isn't just the popular stereotype found in the pages of campus novels of the bookish but socially challenged swot or the egomaniac self-publicist that communicates his or her elevated status at every available opportunity. No, it's not simply that university teachers get a bad press. Academics themselves don't much like other academics, and often feel deep estrangement from their colleagues as people. Perhaps part of the problem is that our forms of self-presentation are tied to the modern academic desire to be taken seriously – that is, the embodiment of entrepreneurialism, 'being smart' and 'world-class' braininess. This means many of our most appealing human qualities are kept hidden like closely guarded secrets. We are always doing our best not to give too much away.

Today I went to a meeting hosted by a national research council. It invited grant holders past and present to come together to discuss a research programme and to 'network'. All of the thirty or so academics present were successful people from a wide variety of disciplines. The facilitator suggested that in order to get to know each other we go around the room and introduce 'yourself, your respective projects, say something about what you want out of the day'. Then, finally, he suggested, 'say something about you that others may not be aware of'. 'Oh no,' I whispered to myself as a collective groan of self-consciousness seemed to rumble around the room.

We started with the visiting speaker from the research council who gave an impressive account of his credentials but chose a diversionary tactic when it came to saying something about himself. 'Something about me? Well, I've never been on X Factor.' I was next in line and said, 'I haven't been on X Factor either but I am a working musician.' As more people introduced themselves a picture emerged of the secret lives of academics. A young women from the research council said, 'My passion is Tudor history.' Another said rather solemnly, 'I am a bee keeper.' Among the group there were also allotment holders, chicken breeders and people who had recently taken up tango dancing. A folk musician said she'd not long ago performed at a prestigious venue in Lancaster and a portly and bespectacled senior professor told us, 'My claim to fame is that in the 60s I gave Brian Jones of the Rolling Stones guitar lessons – not that it did him much good.' A woman in perfect BBC received pronunciation said, 'You wouldn't know it from my accent but I am Glaswegian.' Another member of the group told us she was an opera singer while a younger female academic said that surfing trips to Cornwall in a yellow camper van provided her way to escape the pressures of academic life. My favourite moment was when a seemingly austere middle-aged academic confessed that he had 'been known to juggle and eat fire'. By the end of the 'ice-breaker' my opinion of the exercise had not only thawed but I'd also warmed to my academic colleagues.

During the course of the day I found myself looking around the room smiling to myself as I watched this wonderfully strange collection of bee keepers, folk singers and fire eaters all doing their best to not give up on what American musicians call their 'straight jobs'.

29 November

College Green

College Green is my favourite place at Goldsmiths. This grassy quadrant of open land sits between the Richard Hoggart building – a former Victorian Naval school – and the modern media hub of the new Professor Stuart Hall building. I think lots of campuses have places like this, where the public culture of the institution comes to life. I bump into colleagues and friends walking back and forth along the paths at its edges and catch up on news and gossip. College Green has become Goldsmiths' green beating heart.

It's where graduation is celebrated and twice a year students drink champagne with their loved ones in the marquees erected especially for the occasion. Also, weather permitting, students sit on the grass and celebrate messily the end of something important with cold beers. At lunch in the summer, administrative staff sun themselves on College Green while eating their sandwiches. It wasn't always this way. In the 1980s the area was known as the 'backfield' and students wouldn't venture there much except for football training. After the Stuart Hall building was finished it seemed as if the social centre of gravity of the whole university moved beyond the Richard Hoggart building to the College Green.

Today it was the memorial ceremony celebrating the life of Stuart Hall. I saw Dick Hebdige, author of the classic study *Subculture: The Meaning of Style*, at the memorial. Dick was a student of both Hoggart and Hall. He told me that Richard Hoggart had interviewed him at the University of Birmingham where he applied to study English as an undergraduate. 'I did a bloody awful interview,' he said. 'Embarrassing.' But Hoggart saw something in the awkward young Londoner and offered him a place. Dick then stayed on in Birmingham and worked closely with Stuart Hall during the heyday of the Centre for Contemporary Cultural Studies.

On this sad afternoon 900 people gathered at the Quaker House in central London to remember Stuart Hall's life. As we waited to go in for the ceremony, Dick said how right it was that Goldsmiths' main teaching buildings are named after his former teachers. 'Not quite under one roof' as he put it but their names capture symbolically so much of the spirit of the place. He then turned and said with a wry chuckle, 'Perhaps they should bury us on College Green.' We laughed. It was the kind of laugh that you share to puncture deep sadness. 'Perhaps they should,' I replied. 'Perhaps they should.'

Meeting John Berger

The blueness of John Berger's eyes is striking even from the back of the ICA cinema. He is here tonight at the Institute of Contemporary Arts in central London to talk about translation with his friend and fellow translator Lisa Appignanesi. In Britain, Berger is mostly remembered for his 1972 television series *Ways of Seeing* and the classic book of art criticism that accompanied it. Strangely he is much better known as a literary and political figure in Europe and Scandinavia. Born in Stoke Newington, north London, on Guy Fawkes' day in 1926, he moved to France in the early 1960s and made a conscious choice to become a European writer, publishing nearly thirty books, ten of them novels, as well as poetry.

He has returned to London to talk about his translation of Nella Bielski's novel *The Year is '42* that he worked on with Lisa Appignanesi. The book is an elegiac and subtle tale of people besieged by war in Europe under Nazi rule. 'I translated the book because I wanted it to be read,' says Berger with his trademark directness. 'It is not a French book but a book in French.' Nella Bielski is sitting in the front row. She was born in Ukraine but lives in Paris. It becomes immediately clear that the translation of the book is an exercise in smuggling stories across the borders of language from Russian into French and then English.

Berger's thinking is characterized by carefully chosen words; the sell-out crowd hangs on every single one. Listening to him one is struck by the fact that we live in a culture that speaks too quickly and thinks carelessly. Lisa Appignanesi asks him to summarize the book. He takes his time; he pauses and sighs, 'Oohh K.' He cups his forehead in the palms of his hands covering his eyes. Then the silence is broken irritably, 'No . . . this is impossible, I mean I am here – the translator. Nella is there – the writer. It is impossible for me to summarize while she sits there.' Instead he reads, but the reading is much more like a dramatization than merely reading the words aloud.

When the reading is over Berger tells the audience, 'Translation is a secondary activity.' He stands before a huge white screen and draws two invisible squiggly, parallel lines horizontally. He explains that the lines represent a single sentence and a translation of the sentence into another language. The project of translation for him is not simply a matter of finding corresponding words across the surface of the language – that is, between the lines he has drawn. The audience looks on intently at the visual illustration Berger is making with his finger, yet bizarrely there is nothing to see on the blank white screen. He explains that the true challenge of translation is to reach for the inarticulate human experience that is behind language, behind the screen. This lived reality needs to be rendered within the language of the translation and not simply by finding words that correspond to the literal meaning.

At this point there is more reading, this time a poem: first, it is read in Russian by Nella, then in French by Lisa and finally in English by John. The rhythm of the poem somehow communicates its quality of feeling and emotion, regardless of whether we understand the words or not. The clocks are

Meeting John Berger

slowed down as we listen, almost to the point of timelessness.
It occurs to me that all good poetry does this; it stops time.
'Listening is what is important. The listening to a story is primary, the listening is always primary,' Berger says. All of his
writing is cast through such careful listening.

Berger turns his attention to the language of politics.

> The situation of the world today is where the words that
> politicians say and the words the media use make no sense
> at all. The powerful's speech is corrupted in referential
> terms. 'Democracy', 'terrorism' – they are all corrupted.
> We can say, 'We don't use those words because they shit
> up everything.'

The phrase is awkward, perhaps revealing he is someone who
lives outside his mother tongue. On the table in front of Berger
is a copy of Michael Moore's book *The Official Fahrenheit 9/11
Reader*. Berger wrote a passionate defence in *The Guardian* of
Moore's film about 9/11 as 'a work inspired by hope', praising
its director as a 'people's tribune'.

It is just days after George Bush's re-election in 2004.
Moore's reader begins with the piece written by John Berger
but its presence there on the table is a reminder of the magni-
tude of Bush's triumph. Berger says that the political struggle is
sometimes in the nature of language, in defending the integrity
of words and their meaning. 'This is still important – more than
ever. The world has descended to a situation where the way
politicians speak about the world makes no sense at all to the
people who live on the planet now. It is why it is important to
go on talking and writing.'

A final reading and this time one of Berger's own stories.
'This is a story about your city and mine,' he says. He reads
a description of the train sidings at Willesden Junction seen
through the eyes of a young boy. The sound of Berger's voice is
like a lullaby. Halfway through I hear a breathy snore coming

from a heavily pregnant woman sitting behind me. She is not bored but has been charmed to sleep. The applause that meets the story's end wakes her abruptly from the enchantment. There are questions now from the audience. When confronted with an intelligent comment Berger's face lights up. He seems above all animated by beauty in things or in thought.

As the evening draws to a close the audience file out to the bar or make their way home. My friends suggest that we stay and meet him. It is something that I am embarrassed to do. We decide to buy copies of *The Year is '42*. The man who introduced me to John Berger's writing is a translator. It seems fitting to have a copy signed for him. A queue has formed in the bar. John Berger is speaking energetically with each person and he is generous with his time. I remember that Kingsley Amis once commented that in the full flow of conversation John Berger's hands look like 'two warplanes in a dog fight'.

The queue shortens. It is my friend Vicky's turn next. She is Greek and Berger tells her his daughter is married to a Greek man. Berger's hands are thick with labour, his finger-nails cracked. They are the hands of typesetter or farmer and not those of a writer. As he says goodbye he stands and kisses Vicky extravagantly on each cheek. It is my turn. He reaches out his hand and the initial caution on his face is somehow disappointing.

I explain that I'd like him to sign a copy of the book for a friend of mine called Stephen who is a translator. 'Do you spell that with a "ph" or a "v"?' he asks. There is no room for the profanity of a spelling mistake. I explain I wanted to ask him how he thinks his writing is affected by living in France and outside the language he writes in. The question somehow gives him another burst of energy and he immediately warms to it.

He takes a long gulp from a glass of red wine and then squeezes his forehead in his palm. 'Well it gives me distance in a way . . . it is refuge from the chatter of the media. English is my mother tongue but at the same time I have a distance from

75

it, which in a way helps me to think clearly. Does that make any sense?' I tell him it does and that since the Iraq war I have felt most at peace when I have been abroad in a non-English speaking environment. 'This has happened to me at least on one or two occasions when I pass through London,' he says, introducing a new story.

I crouch by the table where he is sitting and signing books and he puts his hand on my shoulder. 'I am in a pub and I am drinking a beer and I am talking to someone about football or something. Then the person with whom I am speaking looks at me and says, "You know you speak English very well."' We both erupt into laughter of the kind that is embarrassingly loud. 'As if they are speaking to a foreigner, a tourist!' he continues, still laughing. There is something telling in that one of the most artful exponents of English prose can be mistaken for a foreigner in his place of birth!

I tell him how much I enjoyed the piece he wrote about Michael Moore's *Fahrenheit 9/11*. Had he ever met Moore? 'No, I haven't met him but I had a long conversation with him on the phone after that piece was published.' I told him that the night of Bush's re-election I watched the film for the first time and of the desperation that many of us felt after hearing the election result. I find myself asking naively, 'What are we going to do?'

The evergreen radical who will be 90 years old in 2016 replied unflinchingly, 'We must go on, we must go on, that is what Michael Moore would say if he were here.' I produce another book for him to sign. This time it is *A Seventh Man*, his classic study of migration in Europe. 'Could you sign this one for me?' He asks my name. John Berger returns my books and I thank him. I turn back the cover as I turn away. In scratchy blue ink the inscription reads:

For Les – and the language we share!
With best wishes, John Berger.

An Education of Sorts

I was standing in front of the House of Commons with my 17-year-old daughter Stevie just before the Commons vote on the proposal to increase university tuition fees threefold was announced on 9 December 2010. She turned to me and said: 'It's so strange there are men just over there in Parliament right now deciding my future.' For her I think being there that night and sensing the atmosphere sour in the air after the vote was, well . . . an education! We watched on an iPhone over the shoulder of a young man as the votes were announced. Seeing the riot police fully engaged and state power laid bare was a flashback to the 1980s for me and for her a flash-forward. The consequences will be severe for an entire generation.

My head of department commented in a staff meeting earlier the previous week that 'we are presiding over our own privatization'. The Conservative/Liberal Democrat coalition will end the public funding of university teaching with the result that tuition fees will double or even treble. Before the demonstration had even started to disperse the police made pronouncements about 'outside troublemakers' but all that was so out of step with the anger and frustration of the crowd. Recently they have supplanted this 'troublemakers' and 'agitators' line with crocodile tears about middle-class students from 'respectable families' who have ruined their futures through being involved in violence and attacks on property.

There were lots of groups of young people from Lewisham, south London and Tower Hamlets, east London, standing close by. It seemed so clear that the anger crossed the lines of class and colour. I'm not sure how much that has been noted elsewhere. We got away from the police's 'kettling' tactics – that is, confining demonstrators in restricted areas – and the lines of riot police with batons and shields. We bumped into a sociology graduate just behind the Cenotaph. He'd had a conversation in the middle of a kettle with one of the riot police. The officer complained: 'Don't you think we have kids too?' To which the young sociologist said: 'Why don't you put down your shield and let us out then?'

We talked about it. Of course, the officer's individual opinions are an irrelevance. He is choreographed and marshalled by power to hold the rest of us in place, violently reminding anyone who oversteps with a flick, or a full clout, of the baton. There were certainly moments of carnivalesque in the midst of it all, but the thing that has come up time and time again from people I spoke to afterward is the sense of fear and being terrified. The police claim constantly that their actions were reasonable and were made in the name of defending the streets of London – echoing power's *cri du cœur* 'society must be defended'.

Class Mobility

I have always enjoyed the prospect of visiting schools and talking about university education. I remember a particular session that took place in the late nineties that is relevant to the current debate about the rising cost of education. It's a wet, cold Monday morning in south London. A class of Year 11 sociology students awaits the arrival of the lecturer from the university college up the road.

The working-class students of all shades who sit before me are a good sample of the kind of young people that successive governments have tried to lure into higher education through widening participation initiatives. None of them has family members at university. As I prepare to deliver the pitch on why going to university is a good idea, I see out of the corner of my eye a student staring blankly at a window made opaque by condensation.

Doing these sessions is always challenging and rewarding. Increasingly though my enthusiasm is tempered by doubt. I was the first in my family to get a degree and by a twist of fate I now teach in the place that I studied at almost three decades ago. As much as my generation owes a debt to the university as a place of new opportunities and fresh horizons, it is nothing in comparison to what this class will owe in financial terms if they embrace the same opportunity. A three-year degree will leave them with a debt of tens of thousands of pounds. Regardless, the group on this particular occasion listens with courtesy to my invitation to think sociologically.

At the end of the session I packed up my papers. But I couldn't get a troubling question out of my mind. If I had been faced with the same choice as these students would I have taken the financial gamble and applied to university? In all honesty, I don't think I would have. We are told that poorer students will get 'special treatment' and financial assistance. Yet at the same time low income families are placed in a situation where the size of the educational price tag is simply too much of a risk. Claire Callender has argued that the fear of student debt inhibits widening access to university. As she herself has noted, despite this there has been a measure of success in widening student participation and the introduction of student fees that were implemented in 2004 did not halt this.

In 2010 HEFC reported 'young people living in the most disadvantaged areas who enter higher education has increased by around +30 per cent over the past five years'. However, according to Sir Martin Harris, Director of Fair Access, for the top third of selective universities, the proportion of disadvantaged students 'remained almost flat'. There may be an increased measure of access to higher education but there has been little change with regard to where the most advantaged students go to university. The choices students make according to Claire Callender and Jonathan Jackson: 'reflect their material constraints as well as their cultural and social capital, social perceptions and distinctions, and forms of self-exclusion – all of which are class bound'.

In 2010 the new Conservative and Liberal Democrat government trebled university fees at a single stroke. They protested that provision is being made for the poorest students to ensure they can access a university education. There is something very Victorian about the way Liberal Democrat and Conservative politicians refer to the image of the clever but excluded poor students of Bermondsey and elsewhere. It is precisely the politician's privilege that makes them unable to face up with sober senses to what they are doing.

Hand-outs reinforce class distinctions rather than blur them; they ease the guilt of the giver while reducing the recipient to a 'hard luck' case. The key thing that is left out of the ongoing furore about student finance is the emotional politics of class and relative poverty. Class mobility has always been a precarious trade-off between individual escape and the security of group associations, friends and family. More often than not the price of educational opportunity is cutting class-based cultural affinities and associations. This is what Richard Sennett called 'the hidden injuries of class'. The tools of freedom and opportunity – in this case education – are organized in ways that make them also 'sources of indignity'. The financial premium on education intensifies these emotional dilemmas.

Among most working-class and poor families there is a deep fear of debt. This is more than simply a matter of financial risk, it is an ingrained anxiety about being unable to 'pay your way', as much a cultural phenomenon as an economic fact. During my time as an undergraduate the few working-class students I knew never ran up large bank overdrafts; their grant cheques were meticulously accounted for. Rather, it was the students from moneyed backgrounds who cashed cheques like it was going out of fashion.

The present system of student finance will do nothing to address the fear of debt and the emotional costs of class mobility for students with no family history of going to university. It may also have detrimental effects on racial equity. Poverty is disproportionally black and brown and one consequence of the current system – regardless of the determination within minority communities – is that a multicultural university will be harder to accomplish.

Before leaving the south London students there was time for a question and answer session. I could tell the teacher was edgy. A young woman sitting on the back row held up her hand patiently but was passed over by the teacher. Her vigilance was rewarded with the last question. Cutting to the bottom line she asked, 'Sir, how much do you earn?' I blathered on for a few seconds saying 'it's not just being about the money'. Her hand went up slowly again as if hoisting the flag of my own surrender. 'But, how much do you earn?' I told the inquisitor how much I earned at the time as a junior lecturer. She shrugged her shoulders as if to say, 'You expect us to get up to our eyes in debt for that!'

One way to interpret the withdrawal of public investment in higher education by the Conservative/Liberal Democrat coalition government is that they want British universities to have an American future. Chris Newfield, one of the most insightful commentators on the US academy, pointed out in 2011 that the great lesson of the last thirty years is that tuition fee increases did not fix the financial problems of US universities. Through accessing the University of California faculty reports he calculated that in order to return UC to the level of resources it enjoyed in 2001 it would have to find £25,000 per year – double the charge in 2011. Increasing student fees is not the solution to the problem of how to fund universities. Perhaps, if the universities were within reach of every able young person, all taxpayers might be willing to pay the price.

Bourdieu Behind Bars

The entrance of Her Majesty's Prison Grendon is blocked. An articulated lorry is stuck in the doorway of the main gate. Visitors assembled outside have to wait in the chill of a grey winter afternoon along with the next shift of prison guards. A warden pops his head around the door: 'I am sorry, we'll get you in as soon as we can.' My friend and colleague Joe Baden whispers, 'It's always a bit unnerving when screws are nice to you.' Joe is the coordinator of the Open Book project aimed at encouraging ex-offenders to enter higher education. We are here today to visit a potential student for the scheme, who wrote to Joe from Grendon.

After twenty minutes the lorry makes its escape. The new shift of guards files in and then we are invited through. I look back and at the end of a long line of visitors is a familiar face. 'That's Will Self, the writer,' I tell Joe. 'Yeah, he's Razor Smith's agent – he's visiting him probably.' Smith has fifty-eight criminal convictions and has spent most of his adult life behind bars. He earned his nickname for carrying an open razor as a young teddy boy in London during the 1970s and for his willingness to use it on rivals. Inside he taught himself to read and write and gained an honours diploma at the London

School of Journalism and an A-level in law. He's working on a sequel to his first book *A Few Kind Words and a Loaded Gun* while serving a life sentence for armed robbery.

Inside Joe hands the guard our visiting order and we have to show our passports. Prison is like another country and the guard stares back at us with the cold attention of an immigration officer. I ask if it's OK if I bring in a book for the prisoner; it's one of my own. The guard throws another icy look. 'You can't take anything in.' There's something deeply shocking in that even a book needs a visa to gain entry.

We pass through more security checks and then into a waiting room full of toys and children's books. The guard reminds us that we can only take £10 into the visiting area. The rest of our effects have to be placed in a locker. Behind us the guard asks the next visitor which prisoner they are visiting. 'Smith . . . Noel,' replies Will Self in his unmistakably mellifluous tones. He sits down and waits. Joe asks if he should go and speak to the author about the Open Book scheme. Joe grew up in Bermondsey in the 1970s and by his own admission has 'done a bit' inside. His origins and personal history are carried unmistakably in his voice. Yet Joe has the ability to move in different social worlds without changing or compromising himself. He bowls over to the unsuspecting author. 'Have you got a minute?' 'Sure,' replies Self, looking slightly worried. Joe explains the Open Book scheme: 'It's run by people with histories of offending and addiction – we don't go in for any of that missionary bullshit.' The phrase makes the novelist laugh loudly and he repeats it in his nasal baritone. He tells Joe that he is 'busy with a manuscript until March' but he'd be delighted to come and speak to the twenty-seven students already studying at Goldsmiths as part of the scheme. Joe gives him his card. As they part company the novelist says with a sincerity that is not at all his usual public sardonic manner, 'We'll make it happen – have a good visit.'

We are called through to the visiting area. It looks like a cross between a community centre and a motorway services café. Each table has a number; we are told to wait at Number 6. The door opens and the prisoners file through one by one. A black man in his early 40s walks over to our table. 'You must be Les,' he says and reaches over to shake my hand. Simon has a six-year tariff for malicious wounding. He greets Joe and they go to the café to get a cup of tea and some chocolate. Razor is giving Will Self a hard time about the author's new-grown Elvis sideburns: 'You look like that fucking guy from Supergrass.' I overhear the visitor say self-mockingly, 'You're not doing much for my self-esteem.'

Simon returns and he tells me his story. He grew up in a working-class district in north-west London. 'When I was young my attitude was "You've got something, you don't deserve to have it, so I am going to take it." I didn't care about getting banged and I knew as soon as I got out I'd go back to my old ways.' Grendon is a high security prison that offers offenders a specialized form of 'rehabilitation' that subjects inmates to critical therapy. Prisoners have to face up to their pasts. 'It's not an easy thing to do,' Simon says. 'You have to take responsibility for the people you've hurt.'

Simon started studying sociology as part of an Open University programme. His enthusiasm and love of ideas is immediately evident. I ask him if he has a favourite author or set of ideas:

It would have to be Pierre Bourdieu – you know his thing about cultural capital. I mean all the boys came up to visit me. I says to them, 'What the middle classes have got is not money. No, it's what they give their kids – cultural capital. They take them to the opera; they teach them how to study. You can't buy it and you can't steal it from them.'

Bourdieu Behind Bars

I ask him if sociology has helped him to think about his own past differently.

> Yeah, it has, the ideas have, but mostly it has given me a sense that you have to work at learning. I've got something to work for now and I know when I get out I won't be coming back here or a place like it.

We talk for close to an hour about sociologists from Beck and Giddens to Foucault. I tell him about the book that I had brought for him. He explains that all his books have to be sent via his tutor. As we leave he reaches out his hand again. 'Joe has been like a lifeline to me, he's like my blood and I am grateful to him. I am grateful to you too. I mean no one else has got a lecturer coming up to see them.' We say our goodbyes. Turning away I am choked and humbled by his sincerity. Walking through the prison it is intensely apparent how precious learning is behind bars. We step out into the dim winter afternoon. Joe says, 'I think I've got the greatest job in the world. It gives me hope doing these visits, not just for the individuals but everyone around them.' Higher education does work for ex-prisoners. When they get involved in undergraduate study they simply don't re-offend. There are very few cases of re-offending in the Open Book scheme. Today, I put Simon's book in the post; he should receive it before Christmas. I hope it'll be useful to him when he starts his degree course at Goldsmiths, University of London.

New Year's Honours

Established members of the professoriate might be tempted to look expectantly at their letterbox as the end of the calendar year approaches. They hope that a royal communiqué will drop onto their doormat asking if they would accept an honour from the Queen if they were offered one. It's become routine for the names of academics, sociologists and even anti-establishment radicals to be included on the New Year's honours list. Names of campus luminaries appear often sandwiched between high-ranking policemen, managers of a royal household or actors and pop stars. For esteemed academics – like contemporary court poets – the temptation of a knighthood or an OBE, or the elevated title of Dame is simply too much to resist.

Honours come in different forms. The title of Knight or Dame goes back to the medieval period. This explains why knighthoods are conferred by a touch on the shoulder by the royal sword. Others like an OBE or MBE are more recent and have their origin in the British Empire. During the First World War King George V created the honours system to reward contributions to the war effort at home. It is for this reason that they are called Orders of the British Empire, be it

Commander (CBE), Officer (OBE) or Member (MBE). Prime Minister David Cameron's nostalgia for these imperial honours is such that he reinstated the British Empire Medal in 2012, which had been scrapped twenty years earlier.

Today people have to be nominated for an honour, which is in turn evaluated by the various honours committees covering everything from the economy to the arts. Here civil servants, independent advisors and politicians make recommendations for the award of honours to be approved by the Prime Minister and ultimately by the Queen.

Don't get me wrong I have nothing against rewarding citizens for good work – I understand why people who have run hospital trusts or musicians from the wrong side of the tracks are lured to accept an OBE. But for academics it seems they are simply status adornments like medals to be pinned after their name, perhaps alongside their British Academy fellowship. Such baubles smack of an imperial melancholia that haunts British society and indeed university common rooms. How can any intellectual worth his or her salt accept an award that ends with the word 'Empire'?

It is for good reason that many in good conscience have refused to accept them. Stuart Hall turned down both a knighthood and a peerage, as did Richard Hoggart, although, as Alan Bennett – who declined a knighthood – commented, making a public fuss can also smack of 'swanking about it'. The right thing to do in reply to such an offer is perhaps to scribble quietly 'thanks but no thanks'. Not that I have, of course, needed to do this, but I did receive an email today that was a kind of New Year's Honour of sorts.

The email came from a University Campus Suffolk (UCS) student called Samuel Clark whom I had met briefly earlier in the year. He'd attached a copy of an assessment he'd written, a critical review on one of my books entitled *The Art of Listening*. The book had been assigned by Shamser Sinha – a friend and colleague – who teaches sociology at UCS. The students had read the book a chapter each week through the course of the term. The trek to Ipswich to speak to them about the book and their imminent assignment seemed like the least I could do in return for such a compliment. Samuel explained that our discussion prompted him to email:

> The session made me reflect on how important your book has been for me, and immediately reminded me of a passage on the back cover of Marshall Berman's *Adventures in Marxism* that I recently read:

> 'I feel like one of those people whose life is adventures in Marxism. I'm fifty years old, and since I spent my life as a construction worker raising a family, I'm at this stage still in college . . . Your book was inspiring to me because it reminded me of why I made the sacrifices I did to get an education . . . the sheer joy of learning about ideas and the hope that education can make some kind of a difference. The great thing about your approach to Marx is that you show that theory and the world of ideas can be exciting and intellectually rich, but also relevant to all workers, blue collar or otherwise.'

> Personal letter to the author from Scott Smith, construction worker and student (Pittsburgh).

> This passage describes the same feeling I have, when reflecting on what your book has meant to me. I am 28 now and in the final year of my undergraduates degree at UCS. Since leaving school at 17 (dropping out of sixth form after one year), I have worked as a labourer, taking jobs wherever I could. I have two young daughters, and with my partner raising the children, was struggling to find work during

the economic decline. I believed this to be all there was, never imagining there could be an alternative for me. I decided (reluctantly) to consider further education. I doubted my decision until five-to-midnight on the final cut off day, to submit my application; no A levels, no real expectation to get in. By some miracle I did, but my introductory lectures on Marx, Durkheim and Weber had me questioning my decision. I thought about quitting, I was never going to get my head around this complicated theory – I just couldn't see past the jargon. In my first lecture with Shamser however, he held up a book, *The Art of Listening*, which he recommended we all read as an introduction to 'a different kind of Sociology'. It was the first book I had read in ten years. It immediately resonated on a level I had never before experienced, much like Scott when he read Marshall's work, it opened up a whole new dimension. It was relevant to me as a 'blue collar' worker, but also possessed a scope equipped to illuminate the hidden corners of the world. I am glad it was the first book I read, because it laid the foundation for my conception of Sociology, what it is and what it is for.

Samuel's message – accepted gratefully – is the finest reward any university teacher or academic could hope to receive. There are no better words than his to express why I think what we do matters. The value he found in reading my book and thinking about it is expressed so eloquently. Such an acknowledgment is treasured beyond titles, honours, university research rankings or even scores in the national student survey.

Spring Term

The Diary Disease

Clifford Geertz commented that a diary is always in danger of feeding an appetite for salaciousness, and the confession of personal secrets. This he called the 'diary disease' and while this diary is a reflection about academic life, I hope it isn't infected with the malaise that Geertz diagnoses so ably. My intention was never to write some kind of campus exposé. It is not intended either as an exercise in 'professional impression management' which conveys tiring self-importance or an 'advertisement for myself' to use Norman Mailer's telling phase.

Writing creates a world of thought that is both solitary and still and yet is not lonely or isolated. Zygmunt Bauman describes this well in his book *This is Not a Diary*, the title of which communicates his own scepticism about the dangers of the diary disease. For him, writing is not just a matter of reporting life but a way of living life. 'A day without scribbling feels like a day wasted or criminally aborted,' he writes. Turning on his computer and opening up Microsoft Word is the start of a conversation with others. Rather than documenting a single life Bauman's anti-diary shuttles between a description of events unfolding in the society and his own reflections on how to come to terms with them.

The Diary Disease

I have tried to reduce the risk of the diary disease in a similar way, through focusing on small experiences with students and staff on campus and connecting them to larger issues relating to the ethics and conduct of intellectual life. The aim is not merely to counteract the dangers of solipsism inherent in the diary format but to convey an appreciation and recognition of the people – students, lecturers, administrators, receptionists, porters, security guards – that make a university work.

Remembering Paul

University teachers shouldn't survive their students. This isn't a matter of thinking of our students as the medium through which to secure immortality or as disciples who will carry our wisdom beyond our lifetime. Neither is this about securing what some writers and thinkers call 'a legacy'. No, there is something wicked and evil about the extinguishing of a young life in the middle of a life-changing experience like studying at university. Our students' enthusiasm and sincerity can be exasperating and yet they often gift us a reminder not to let our most cherished commitments slip away.

'It will only take about twenty minutes to a half an hour,' Paul said when we arranged to meet and talk about his Deptford Town Hall radio project. It wasn't the first time we'd spoken, but it was to be the first of many conversations about our shared interests in empire, racism, music and cultural politics. It will be of no surprise to anyone who knew Paul Hendrich that the twenty minutes actually stretched to well over three hours of intense but joyful discussion. Paul not only liked to talk – much more, he liked to listen.

One of his special qualities was the time he took to pay attention to others, to care about them. He made time for people, often enabling them to take time to think more carefully for themselves and about themselves. That afternoon he asked me, 'What is it that you think you are doing with your work – not just your writing but also your teaching?'

I thought for more than a moment; his questions often had that effect. 'I think my job is to make myself obsolete.' He turned his head; the expression on his face was slightly pained, as if hearing the suggestion almost hurt physically. His friends and loved ones will know exactly the look I am talking about.

'No? Really? You don't mean that,' Paul replied. I assured him that I did. 'I think my job is to carry ideas, problems and political commitments as far as I can – and then let other people pick them up, make them their own in ways that are beyond my capacity.' He smiled, that huge smile of his, and nodded with approval. Our meeting would have probably gone on much longer than three hours had the Goldsmiths porters not insisted that it was time to lock up and go home.

Paul's death robbed us of his extraordinary ability to give and take time. At his memorial in Goldsmiths' Great Hall, a young refugee whom Paul had worked with spoke about the way he 'always seemed to have time for you'. Paul's life is a much needed example of the best values of education, values that are in danger of being lost in the haze of academic self-ishness and pressure. Alpa, his PhD supervisor, told me that Paul had spoken often of our talks. 'He wanted to be like you,' she said. Hard words to hear – I certainly didn't deserve that admiration. On the contrary, I left the Great Hall that sunny afternoon feeling a desperate desire to be more like him.

Paul was playful in even the most serious things, a kind of theatrical seriousness. His politics and his projects were often coloured by a capacity to make the most terrible issues fun, while at the same time naming shameful historical injustices. His political style had a nod to Situationism, but also a humorous wink of comic genius. The Deptford Pirates project and his work around the bicentenary of the abolition of the slave trade are good examples of this combination. I don't think I really appreciated this during his lifetime, but it is a lasting memory now. Less the beach underneath the cobblestones, than a pirate's treasure buried somewhere underneath the tarmac of south London's A2 that passes by Goldsmiths and the road that links the city to the green hinterlands of Kent.

He was also a gentle person; it was part of his general openness to people and life's prospects. He was a living refusal of the urban maxim, 'The world will make you hard.' No, the world doesn't make us hard, it makes us soft, vulnerable and lays us bare to the steel structures of modern life and hatreds that are set hard in our city like concrete. Paul refused to live life in that way; he just refused to be hardened. He rode his bicycle and he was crushed by the juggernaut of metropolitan hardness.

Returning home after his memorial, a wonderful celebration of Paul's personality and his many qualities, my daughter asked, 'What is wrong, Dad?' I said softly, turning away, unable to hide rheumy eyes, 'You shouldn't survive your students, you shouldn't survive your students.'

Not that Paul was ever a student of mine. Perhaps we studied some of the same questions and struggled together with similar problems. He should have taken my place. I know he would have found answers with more grace, style and humour. Those gifts have been stolen from us, along with the many other wonderful things that he would have inevitably scattered through our lives. We can cherish his example and his memory, but there is no gilding over the sadness of a talent, and a life, cut short so pointlessly.

Recognition

I was struck today by the realization that while academics ag-
onize about their status and standing, intellectual recognition
is very fleeting. Visiting a University of London college I overheard one of the faculty say, 'My work isn't really recognized
enough.' This common academic complaint belies the fact
that even the greatest thinkers are humbled by time.

At the beginning of Pierre Bourdieu's *Sketch for a Self-Analysis*
there is a portrait of philosopher Jean-Paul Sartre. Seen through
the eyes of the young École Normale Supérieure student, Sartre personifies the 'total intellectual'. Master of philosophy, literature, history and politics, Sartre is surrounded by a legion
of young radical acolytes. To his adoring young followers the
existentialist author had written the last word on the human
condition in books like *Nausea* and *Being and Nothingness*. Reflecting on this, Bourdieu – never one to follow intellectual
fashion – is disparaging of 'Sartre worship', and an intellectual
style that 'encourages a self-confidence often verging on the
unself-consciousness of triumphant ignorance'.

A very different portrayal of Sartre is found in Jean Améry's
book *On Aging*. Through his protagonist – referred to as A. –
we meet Sartre speaking to another packed room of students,

but this time towards the end of his life. For many years A. held Sartre in great esteem. It is not the topic of the lecture that draws A. but simply the fact it is Sartre who is giving it.

A. had followed Sartre's work for over thirty years as a dedicated reader and pupil. In fact A. had heard Sartre before in the springtime of 1946 when his intellectual hero had 'exuded a strong physical force of attraction, something virile and powerful'. In the great hall of a large Western university, Sartre has been transformed by the passage of time. A. is shocked by the physical decline: 'My god, now he has become frail, tired gentleman, a senile man with a flaccid, pale grey face, an emaciated body, and an exhausted, rattling voice, he has become old with time weighing inside him.' The transitory nature of academic power or intellectual authority is one of the implications of Améry's parable. Perhaps, if academics kept this in mind we might be less prone to episodes of intellectual arrogance, snobbery and self-aggrandisement. Améry points out here that time will humiliate even the greatest mind.

However, for A. it is not just Sartre's physical demise that is troubling. For the aged Sartre offers a stunning performance on the night in question, outlining a sharp justification of the Russell Tribunal's case against the Vietnam war. 'They cannot know that the esteem they display for the aged man who snatches up his papers and makes for the exit on his tiny feet is "dis-esteem" and a malicious condemnation,' reflects A. This is because the young admirers carry within them the living embodiment of the 'anti-Sartre' – that is, their young bodies will outlive his old failing one. As a result A. views the acolytes' tribute as 'sombre, like an obituary. In it they anticipate the philosopher's death. Applause. Bravo, bravo. But now to ourselves the world! A good and great old man. After him greater and better ones are coming and we, the young, will be there with them. The gigantic hall empties.'

I have witnessed this syndrome in people who rush to hear

and see a great thinker because they think s/he might be fatally ill. There's something insulting in such morbid sentiments: 'Must get to see X because it might be the last chance.' This is the equivalent of behaving badly at a funeral except the person whose death is anticipated is standing there before the audience at the lectern. I recall a renowned academic writer well into his 70s comment with bewilderment that every time he speaks in public he is filmed or recorded. Curiously he has never received copies of the recordings; they were evidently not intended for him. Rather, they are taken for a future that does not include him, except as a ghostly ornament embalmed with digital fidelity.

In another way, Sartre's acolytes might think that he belongs exclusively to them. To say you have 'grown up with a thinker' is to make a privileged claim to their ideas. There are many people who act like this with regard to great thinkers like Bourdieu or Foucault, but such claims miss another twist. All books are spectral dossiers, time-lapsed thoughts that have been written down. As a consequence, reading is a kind of possession, as the words inhabit us as much as we inhabit them.

Literary work is secure because it outlives not only its authors but also its students. There are no readers beyond the time of a book. Books and the thoughts contained within them are not the exclusive property of any generation. This is perhaps the writer's ultimate reprisal.

Holding the Fort

My daughter came into work with me today. Walking past the rows of empty offices she said: 'Your work must be a lonely place – there never seems to be anyone here!' Academics are absentee workers. This is why high profile 'big names' are infrequently the people that really make universities work as organizations. In part this is due to the fact that in order to inflate one's name intellectually and in terms of standing (and too often self-importance) it is necessary to be missing. It means having to travel to give that international keynote address and be out and about in the world of ideas. I am as guilty of this as anyone else.

Absenteeism is a hallmark of being in demand. This is called 'dissemination' and 'impact' in the rhetoric of grant applications, that is, to scatter the academic self in order to propagate ideas and harvest citations of one's published work. For this reason the office of an academic 'high flyer' can look like an intellectual bedsit that is only intermittently inhabited, home only to books overtaken by academic fashion – a kind of intellectual equivalent of putting your furniture into storage.

It's a curious, perhaps even a unique thing in the world of employment, that academic employees often try to avoid going to work in order to work. This is why university departments are sparsely populated, even at the busiest times of the academic year. To the uninitiated this seems preposterous: 'Why aren't you at work if you are working?' Non-appearance is not indicative of indolence but the real labour of mind takes place elsewhere and certainly not 'in the office'. I don't know many lazy academics. This might seem contradictory. Our minds are rarely off our work but not necessarily on what's going on in the department office. How do universities function if academic members of staff remain institutionally absent?

The smooth running of universities – even the most prestigious ones – depends on those who are left behind. Usually referred to as 'support staff', as Mary Evans has pointed out they are a predominantly female workforce of secretaries, administrators, web designers, accountants, human resources specialists and clerical workers. Alongside them is a legion of working-class men who serve long hours as porters, gardeners, maintenance staff and security guards, often over-qualified migrant labourers doing these jobs to earn money while dreaming of a better future. Without them there would be no university. Academics would have nowhere to teach their students or return to from their adventures on the frontiers of knowledge.

They are the university's public characters but many of them often have interesting lives off campus. Take Trevor, for example: his job is to greet and he assists visitors to the college at its main entrance. A ceaselessly patient and welcoming person, he is almost singlehandedly responsible for the positive experience guests have visiting Goldsmiths. Most of the people he encounters there are unaware of the fact that he is also an accomplished bass guitarist who has recorded and performed with jazz and soul artists on prestigious stages from London to New York.

Attempts to bridge the academic/support staff divide contain a sometimes touching pathos. As a student, I looked on disparagingly at professors who, to prove that they hadn't lost the 'common touch', would joke with the porters as they arrived with impossibly large bunches of keys to lock up the seminar room. Support staff on the receiving end of much more brutal forms of academic self-importance and snobbery might say that being patronized in doomed attempts to bridge the university's class structure is the least of their problems.

I have always had a strangely Fordist habit of actually 'going to work'. As a consequence, my workplace friends and acquaintances have often been 'non-faculty'. This is not to claim some perverse street credibility or the delusion of being outside of what is being described here. It is simply to suggest that it is deeply sobering to listen to how they view the behaviour of academics. Some say there is a stark division on campus between the 'intellects' who regard each other as peers – whether loved or loathed – and the 'clericals' who are non-persons disregarded or disparaged.

As the minute-takers and intellectual non-combatants they are witness to bickering in meetings, paddies of high moral principle and the worst cases of academic vanity. Highly intelligent people are reduced to acting like squabbling children at the seaside in 'red bucket' syndrome: 'I want to build my sandcastle with the red bucket not the yellow one!' That is how it often seems to bewildered secretaries and administrators who have to manage what one friend described as the full 'cornucopia of personality disorders'. More disturbing is the double standard with regard to workplace etiquette where support staff are ignored in ways that a faculty colleague simply would not be.

A former secretary of an academic department offered three pieces of advice (her own three 'red buckets') for academic staff:

1. Before you ask a question of an administrator, check the emails they have sent you in the last week or so. The fact that you have suddenly thought of that question probably means that a section of your brain was prompted by an email you've received that answers all your queries perfectly, but you didn't read it at the time.

2. If you ask an administrator to do something, please trust them to do it. The fact they haven't done it within two to three minutes of you sending the email or speaking to them does not mean they are ignoring you. In fact, if you check your emails you will probably find that they were waiting for a vital piece of information from you. What they don't appreciate is slogging through your rambling prose/random, seemingly unconnected words (please delete as appropriate), finding your response to the question they asked you four days ago, doing the task and then being informed by someone else that the job is already done because you decided to do it yourself anyway.

3. Administrators are not sitting twiddling their thumbs and filing their nails waiting for you to come to them with that thing you should have done last month and now needs to be sorted by tomorrow. Do not expect to be greeted with a smile in this circumstance. Administrators tend to plan their time which means if you have come to them for help because you have failed to do so, they will then be under even more pressure than the students/ university/HoD/other members of staff/external agencies already put them under. Realize that an emergency for you will mostly be very low down the list in the grand scheme of things. Oh, and when they have sorted it out for you, a smile and a thank you wouldn't kill you!

This is one side of the story.

Others will say that faculty and support staff collaborate amicably most of the time. The ivory tower is divided to its very foundations by stark class and status divisions. Academics might complain about the inappropriate loquaciousness and strange preoccupations of their non-academic colleagues but it bears remembering that they witness and in large part tolerate our own strange habits. Regardless, it needs to be remembered that in the absence of us faculty it is non-academic staff who actually get things done and make universities work.

Academic Uses and Abuses of Twitter

'Modesty was not [Auguste] Comte's strong suit,' writes Wolf
Lepenies. Comte, the architect of the cold science of positiv-
ism was as much an ascetic as he was a workaholic. Regardless
of his prodigious work rate, Lepenies points out in his history
of the rise of sociology that even Comte's most devoted followers would concede that he was not a great writer. In his
will, Comte decreed that after his death his house should be
undisturbed and left as it was when he worked in it. Visitors
today can still see the desk that stands against a wall where he
coined the term 'sociology'. Above it is a large mirror as wide
as the writing desk. As Comte wrote a sentence he could pause
and look up and admire himself. There is perhaps no better
symbolic image of academic vanity than Comte's mirror.

    After reading this I felt the urge to share it. Having become
a devotee of the social network Twitter, I decided to send a
message. Twitter allows short messages of 140 characters to
circulate among your network of followers. The structure is
simple: you access the messages of the people you are following on your phone or laptop and reply or 'like' them. In turn
other members of the network can follow and reply to yours
and this is how the network of connections is built. So, I sent

out a message describing Comte's mirror. Almost immediately I received a reply from @AviGoldberg who wrote wryly, 'Today, he'd check Twitter?' Avi put his finger on something. In the digital age, has Twitter become a new medium for academic vanity, the digital equivalent of Comte's mirror?

I started to notice Twitter being used only as a broadcast medium by some 'celebrity academics' who were just advertising themselves: 'something else written by me', 'a brilliant review of me', 'PhD scholarships that I will handing out', etc. Universities are doing this too where their Twitter feed is little more than a long and tiresome exercise in institutional boasting. The lack of interest in dialogue or interaction is often revealed where there is a disparity between the large numbers of followers a particular academic star might have and the small number of people that are actually following.

Another criticism is that academic Twitter feeds the culture of audit within university life through a kind of enforced visibility. Academics increasingly have to demonstrate and evidence their profile, audience and impact on the world. Large numbers of Twitter followers provide a convenient metric of academic celebrity and standing. Caroline Knowles and Roger Burrows write:

> In this context the high vis academic tweets, blogs or otherwise makes visible every thought and activity in the new domains in which value is judged. Department Websites, Twitter accounts and blogs 'buzz' with our labours in ways that can be seen by ever-new audiences. It's not what we do that matters but what we are seen to do by those who count or who can be counted.

More than this, there is a shadow game of academics watching each other on Twitter to see who is going to blink or react. It seems clear that Twitter has become a new weapon in the dark academic arts. This was particularly evident around the announcement of the results of the 2014 Research Excellence Framework. This can take very different forms. Triumphant Heads of Department or Vice Chancellors gloated on Twitter about the success of their institutions, while other professors tweeted little in order not to draw too much attention because they had sat on the REF panel.

We cannot blame Twitter for academic vanity. Doesn't scholarship contain an inherent conceit as the point of writing anything contains the temerity of the appeal to be read? Twitter allows for that audacious request – contained in all writing – to be circulated at a new scale and frequency. If the hubris of writing in the first place is forgivable then tweeting about it must be equally excusable. Taking all this into account I would like to make a modest defence of academic Twitter.

What I like about academic Twitter is that it allows me to follow the fascinations of others. Tweets are often like signposts pointing to things going on in the world: a great article, an important book, a breaking story. It allows for a circulation of hunches and tips, which is the lifeblood of scholarship. There is something so valuable in the possibility of inhabiting the attentiveness of another writer. All writing does this but the twittersphere offers access to an author's preliminary and ephemeral notes. This is not about 'being them' in some vicarious way but rather an outward looking impulse, finding interest in what they are interested in.

While Twitter offers universities a medium for corporate publicity it can also flatten academic hierarchies. It brings professors into dialogue with GCSE students and provides a medium in which academic researchers can interact with political activists or local councillors. Very often Twitter creates a sphere in which a citizen sociology can come to life, albeit fleetingly. This is particularly the case where tweets are linked to online publications or podcasts that are freely available. It allows for the democratic circulation of ideas outside the expensive pay-walled academic journals.

Twitter can also be a very effective medium to humorously cut academic pomposity down to size. Anonymous feeds like @academicmale fictionally document the worst excesses of academic masculinity. Another very funny account is Shit Academics Say @AcademicsSay which quotes faculty clichés and re-mixes them. These hilarious tweets read like actual overheard senior common room conversations and leave no doubt whose expense the joke is at. They offer compensation to those who otherwise have to suffer in silence the company of such academic personality types.

The openness and permeability of Twitter makes it a power mechanism to reconnect with former students, colleagues or fellow travellers. This has happened to me time and time again. Students have got back in touch via Twitter sometimes after twenty years, often giving inspiring news about how their degrees made a lasting influence and put them on a course in life. It can bring risks and vulnerabilities too, of course. A number of colleagues have needed to find ways to protect themselves from harassment and digital stalking on Twitter. Where people are speaking out on contentious political issues this kind of vulnerability brings real dangers. Twitter can also be a place for reconciliation.

Published writing is indelible – once it is in print you cannot change your mind. Writing fixes thought. While digital communication has similar qualities – there are plenty of cases where tweets have been held against their authors – it does offer the opportunity to augment or revise keyboard judgements. The value of this became clear to me in 2011 when I was just finding my way around Twitter. I received a message from someone who was tweeting from an anonymous account. It read: 'I gave one of your books a really bad review and I just wanted to say that I think you were right. That bad review has given me a lot of sleepless nights.'

I replied to the tweet and said that criticism was part of our vocation and a scholarship without it wasn't worth its salt.

I never found out which review it was or what book had been mauled by it. I am sure it hurt at the time like all bad reviews. This anonymous message was a reminder that even the most avid critics sometimes change their mind. Without Twitter this circuit of communication and the lesson contained within it would not have been possible. It served as a reminder that the critic has to live with the review as much as the author who is dissected by it.

My last defence of Twitter is that it can make scholarship more sociable. This sociability is not always a matter of distraction. Quite the reverse: the academic sociability I am thinking of here produces a kind of collective focus even when our scholarly work is a profoundly individual matter. The best example of this is Dr Siobhan O'Dwyer's Twitter network Shut Up & Write Tuesdays @SUWTues that coordinates writerly discipline among academic researchers.

The idea of writers getting together to focus on writing – hence 'shut up and write' – began in San Francisco. Dr Inger Mewburn – aka the Thesis Whisperer – brought the idea to Australia where Siobhan O'Dwyer participated in 'shut up and write' sessions 'in-person' in Brisbane. She explains: 'One day I tweeted that I was on my way to one of these sessions and one of my followers said she was keen to write that day, so I suggested that I could tweet each time we started and stopped and she could join in virtually. And thus the idea was born!'

Siobhan started Twitter-coordinated Shut Up & Write Tuesdays in late 2013. At first they were weekly sessions where people participated from all over Australia. They tweeted at the start of the session and then signed off with a tweet when they had finished writing. It has been incredibly successful. As well as in Australia, there has been interest in the idea in the UK and other EU states and in the US. The time zone differences made international coordination difficult. The result is that Dr Rebecca Jefferies agreed to host Shut Up & Write Tuesdays

UK and Jen Goff recently expressed interest in hosting Shut Up & Write Tuesdays North America, which both started in 2014.

Under pressure due to the level of interest, Siobhan now limits the sessions in Australia to the first and third Tuesday of every month.

Today writing is something we do individually but not necessarily alone and that is one of the benefits of Twitter and the example of Shut Up & Write Tuesdays emphasizes this point. There is some consolation in the knowledge that there are other writers at their desks just like us struggling to find the right words. While Twitter might be prone to the same kinds of academic vanities that Comte and others indulged in, it also offers the possibility to make thinking more democratic and accessible. It enables thought to move differently and make not just contemporary connections but also links to past students and much wider traces of an academic life that would otherwise remain unknown. All this is no small achievement in just 140 characters.

Generosity as a Strategy for Survival

There are colleagues who view being too positive about the work of other academic writers as Panglossian. As Harvey Molotch once pointed out: 'Sociologists like to eat each other . . . critics by disposition and occupation [they] freely take issue with each other, often ungenerously.' This is because we are valued not for our generosity but for the sharpness of our intellect, for the unflinching nature of our academic judgements. These qualities can be rewarded, for example, by being invited to serve as a judge on panels like those that determine the outcomes of the Research Excellence Framework (REF). Critical edge becomes a badge of excellence, while generosity shows suspicious signs of intellectual feebleness.

In this kind of climate I have come to think that valuing the work of others becomes a way to strike a small blow of munificence against miserliness in academic life. This is not just a matter of being 'nice' to others. Sometimes there are profound divisions and intellectual fault lines that are important to fight over. A university without criticism and argument is no kind of university at all. No, I am thinking more about the pleasure that can be taken in admiring the work of others that you feel animates something important.

114

Machiavelli was of course right to advise in *The Prince* to be wary of flatterers and sycophants. Praise can be manipulative, a way of courting favour: the heart of even the stoniest professional can be melted with a few obsequious words. I am not advocating toadyism but rather generosity in the service of what Russell would have called educated self-interested.

One way of coping with life in the university today is – in part – to trade envy for admiration. It is a lesson that I have learned from some of my feminist colleagues. Intellectual generosity can be a survival strategy and prophylactic against the corrosive aspects of intellectual cruelty that have been institutionalized by the audit culture. Try it. You might never get asked to serve on an assessment panel pronouncing on the intellectual merits of those in your field but maybe you'll feel better about academic life and your place within it.

Professionals and Amateurs

I attended an event today on the future of the British university. In many respects the prospect of the academy looks
gloomy: cuts in public spending leading to educational cuts,
limiting university places, increase of student tuition fees, more
auditing of research 'excellence' and the fear that all this will
lead to redundancies. Beyond these symptoms our consciences are held hostage to the idea that being an intellectual is
reduced to having and keeping an academic job.

So much so that for young PhD students 'research training'
comes to dominate how they encounter the craft of scholarship. Max Weber's suggestion that 'science is a vocation', a
disposition and a way of holding to the world, is translated into
the language of 'professional development' and the acquisition
of a career. As Edward Said commented in his 1993 Reith Lectures: 'The particular threat to the intellectual today, whether
in the West or in the non-Western world, is not the academy,
nor the suburbs, nor the appalling commercialism of journalism and publishing houses, but rather an attitude that I will call
professionalism.'

The world of ideas is reduced to an academic game to be
played with stealth. The life of the mind becomes fixated with

fostering one's career: jobs, promotions, measuring up to performance indicators, publishing in the most prestigious places, aspiring to a 'world class' profile. For Said this results in:

> thinking of your work as an intellectual as something you do for a living, between the hours of nine and five with one eye on the clock, and the other cocked at what is considered to be proper, professional behaviour – not rocking the boat, not straying outside accepted paradigms or limits, making yourself marketable and above all presentable . . .

Appropriate forms of professional behaviour take on a style of self-presentation, from appointments panels to the plenary colloquium but also produce habitual judgements concerning not only what is valuable but also what is valid.

Auditable forms of value (publications, grants, etc.) provide the medium through which we come to see our own worth and that of others. I think it is difficult to remain vigilantly impervious to the occupational modes of evaluation captured in phrases such as 'does this person have enough publications to be entered in the next exercise when research will be evaluated?'

In Said's argument there are three dimensions to the damage that professionalism does to scholarship and thinking. The first of these is the processes of specialization. For him the paradoxical result of the cultivation of research expertise is that it results in anti-intellectualism. Nobel Laureate Konrad Lorenz explains:

> There is a serious danger that the specialist, forced to compete with his colleagues in acquiring more and more specialised knowledge, will become more and more ignorant about other branches of knowledge, until he is utterly incapable of forming any judgement on the role and im-

portance of his own sphere within the context of human knowledge as a whole.

The specialist can go on mining within a very narrow, intellectually fenced-in area without ever being disturbed by the burning issues of the day. 'Specialisation, I have always felt, is laziness,' writes Edward Said abruptly.

However, this does not mean that specialists don't work extremely hard at their vocation. The work that they do, though, is often consumed with defending their area of professional expertise and this is the second damaging feature of professionalism. The studied maintenance of a professional reputation is a time-consuming business and involves the vigilant rebuttal and undermining of any interlopers on your intellectual territory.

Lastly, Said argues that professional intellectuals drift towards power through the enticements of honours or research grants with political strings attached. The result is timidity, a desire not to rock the boat or be too outspoken. Don't do anything that might threaten the next offer to give a conference keynote or the invitation to join an editorial board.

By contrast Said espouses a model of the intellectual as the passionate dilettante or committed dabbler. 'The intellectual today ought to be an amateur' he concluded. Making intellectual life a job has resulted in conventionalism and an aversion to risk-taking. Also, vocational anxiety has stifled the joys and surprises of intellectual exploration. The word 'dilettante' is derived from the Latin *delectare*, to 'delight'.

There is something in Said's attempt to reclaim amateurism for scholarship that offers a corrective to dull academic instrumentality. In today's university many would say that these are luxuries that can only be afforded by a very select few. The appeal to intellectual dilettantism might well turn out to be, as Max Farrar commented in a different context, the 'prerogative of the very successful and the retired'. Equally, amateurism might also be a licence just to do the difficult work of thinking badly or poor intellectual journalism.

However, some of the most lucid writers and witnesses of the twentieth century fit the model being suggested here. Primo Levi, for example, was both a professional chemist and a writer. His profession made him useful to the overseers of the Nazi death camps at Auschwitz during the year he spent in the chemical Kommando. His trade was key to his survival. On his return to Turin, the city where he lived all his life except for the year he spent in Auschwitz, he became a writer in part as a way of reckoning with the time he spent behind barbed wire. He was much more than merely a literary witness to the Nazi holocaust. He wrote novels, journalism and poetry on a wide variety of topics.

Other People's Trades is a collection of Levi's essays originally published in Turin's newspaper *La Stampa*. The pieces range from literary reviews to social observation and philosophical fragments. Although he characterizes himself as 'too much a chemist and a chemist for too long to consider myself a real man of letters', Levi's incursions into the trades of other people are adventures inspired by what he describes as a 'durable fascination of unrequited loves'. He comes to art and literature with the patience and technical precision of a scientist but also writes of science with the flair of a novelist.

Jane Jacobs, author of the classic study *The Death and Life of Great American Cities*, is another example of a compelling writer who was a brilliant amateur. Born in Scranton, Pennsylvania in 1916, Jacobs moved to New York when she was 19. Having completed a stenographer course she found work as a secretary but the work was intermittent and she found herself routinely pounding the New York sidewalks in search of work. Biographer Alice Sparberg Alexiou commented that Jacobs 'found her subjects just by walking about, letting her mind settle wherever it wanted. She would scribble down notes on whatever scraps of paper she had in her purse. Then she would go home and write.'

Jacobs wrote about an incredible range of topics, from the variations in the size of New York manhole covers to the economics of the city's fur business. The articles she wrote appeared in a wide variety of magazines from *Cue* to *Vogue* and led eventually to an associate editor position at a publication called *Architectural Forum*. By this time Jacobs was now a mother raising her children in Greenwich Village, while riding her bicycle to work every day.

Her take on urban change and city life was fashioned not through city plans or academic seminars but from paying close attention to the ebb and flow of neighbourhood life. This sensibility was expressed in an article entitled 'Downtown is for People' that appeared in *Fortune* magazine in 1958. The article was critical of the hubris of architects and the tearing down of old neighbourhoods and the building of huge housing projects. She wrote: 'You've got to get out and walk. Walk, and you will see that many of the assumptions on which the projects are based are visibly wrong.'

Her friends and supporters described her as a 'wonderfully likeable, contentious and opinionated woman', but as Sparberg Alexiou points out the architectural establishment and conservative academic urbanists viewed her as an upstart. Publisher of *Fortune* C.D. Jackson is purported to have asked having read Jacobs' article: 'Who is this crazy dame?' Other commentators dismissed her as a 'housewife' and even one 'without a college degree'.

Regardless, she would go on to complete her classic study of city life in 1961. Part of the reason why *The Death and Life of American Cities* is such an enduring book is because it tells the city's story from the vantage point of the citizen, a Greenwich Village mother who witnesses the street corner ballet first hand. It is this view of the city from the sidewalk or from

Jacobs' bicycle that is so fresh – even now, over fifty years later – and which communicated the social life of cities with vivid clarity.

My last example, poet William Carlos Williams, didn't simply have another trade – he was a doctor in Paterson, New Jersey during the early part of the twentieth century – and through his practice he was drawn into a profound engagement with the lives of others. For Williams the two professions, symbolized in the stethoscope and the typewriter, enhanced each other.

These relationships could be fraught in the midst of the Great Depression of the 1930s and some of his working-class patients were deeply suspicious of him. He was torn about using the lives of the people he attended to as a doctor as a resource for his writing. Yet he was animated by the desire to capture poetically and with sensitivity the texture of working people's lives.

The physician, after a lifetime of careful listening, bore witness to:

> the inarticulate patient [who] struggles to lay himself bare for you, or with nothing more than a boil on his back is so caught off balance that he reveals some secret twist of the whole community . . . It is just a glimpse, an intimation of all that which the daily print misses out or deliberately hides, but the excitement is intense and the rush to write is on again.

The social landscape in which Levi, Jacobs and Williams practised their respective trades is a strong feature of their writing. Their work contains – both implicitly and explicitly – the writers' deep attachment to place. Part of the lesson contained in their books is the importance of maintaining a hinterland beyond the academy. Sociologist Harvey Molotch captured this in his phrase 'going out' which is an appeal to do, live and think adventurously, that is, to become entangled in the life of the city, or a political activity or a cultural field like music or art.

It is not only a choice between being a professional supplicant or cultivating an amateurish conscience but also a matter of having a hinterland in which the imagination can be nourished. In the case of these writers it was their 'day jobs' or their experience living the life they sought to understand that fed their craft as writers. It might be simply a matter of getting out more and following our intellectual passions without the inhibiting sense that we are thinking ourselves out of a job.

Reading and Remembering

If a book really strikes a chord with me I feel like I need to give it to everyone who might appreciate the book in the same way. It's like a compulsion to organize something equivalent to a 'literary potlatch'. Turning the last page of a great read evokes a strong obligation to share it with someone else. This isn't good if your bank balance is on the red side, or if, when you take your credit card out in Waterstones, it groans. Maybe the impulse to share favourite books is, in part, driven by the paradox of reading itself.

Reading is always about listening to that solitary voice in your head that speaks as your eye jumps from sentence to sentence across the page. But the private act of reading is also profoundly about breaking isolation. As Salman Rushdie once put it, a different kind of identity is produced 'as reader and writer merge, through the medium of the text, to become a collective being that both writes as it reads and reads as it writes'. For Rushdie, this is the greatest and most subversive gift offered by a book. Perhaps it is this quality in reading which is a kind of sociability that compels bibliophiles to say 'You have to read this book . . .'

Mitch Albom's wonderful and moving autobiographical

book *Tuesdays with Morrie* is the story of a great teacher –
Morrie Schwartz – who also happened to be a sociologist.
I came upon this book quite by chance. It was the last book
that my mother-in-law, Gill, read before she died after a long
and gruelling illness. She read it in hospital just days before
the end of her life. She loved it and wanted her children to
read it and each member of her family to possess a copy.
Subsequently, her daughter Debbie read it and passed it on.

Rushdie is right when he says there is something surrepti-
tious about the act of reading, but books that have been read
many times carry in them the traces of previous readings.

This can take the form of the invisible thumbprints that
cause wear and tear on the pages themselves, or 'intelligent
graffiti' left in margin notes or in underlined passages. As I
read *Tuesdays with Morrie* I wondered how its previous owners
had written their own feelings of joy, hope, fear and regret
as they read. The book contained no marginalia or scribbled
notes. The imprint of other eyes was left by thumb and finger
marks and pages turned down at the corner.

There are two stories in the book. First is Mitch's story.
It is the tale of a student who encounters a charismatic and
inspiring teacher. Mitch describes the first time he met Morrie
in class. We have all experienced the tentative encounters between staff and students in Week 1, as each test the other out.
Morrie sat in front of the class and read through the register.
He came to the name Mitchell Albom and asked his new student whether he preferred to be called 'Mitch' or 'Mitchell'.
The freshman replied that his friends called him 'Mitch'.

'Well, Mitch it is then,' replied Morrie. 'I hope that one day
you will think of me as your friend.' So begins their relationship.

Mitch does all of Morrie's classes; he is an inspiring teacher
who tries zany things to get through to his students and keep
their interest. Morrie loves to dance and turns up to student
bops in sweatpants and dances emphatically in wild solos to

everything from Jimi Hendrix to Frank Sinatra. Mitch becomes enchanted with Morrie. After three years they do indeed become friends. At graduation he promises Morrie that they will stay in touch, a promise that is broken almost as soon as it is made. They do not see each other or speak until years later.

After trying and failing to become a professional jazz musician, Mitch throws himself into a career in journalism. He becomes a sports writer of national prominence and pursues success in a driven way. Yet, he finds only fleeting fulfilment. Then one night the face of his old mentor appears on the TV screen. Morrie is being interviewed for Ted Koppel's programme *Nightline*, which is something close to the UK's *Newsnight*. Morrie is dying of a terrible wasting disease. The TV programme's headline reads: 'A professor's final course: his own death.' Mitch vows to get back in contact with Morrie and in doing so begins to re-think his aspirations and what his life has become.

The second story, of course, is Morrie's. Morrie was the son of a Jewish immigrant and spent his youth living in a poor neighbourhood in the Lower East Side of Manhattan. He finds his vocation as a teacher. He possessed an incredible capacity to communicate to his students his love of thinking and reading. During the Vietnam War a minor crisis was precipitated because almost an entire class of students in the sociology department was about to fail. They had spent their time on demonstrations, neglecting Durkheim and Weber; Morrie had taught them well. Failure would mean that the male students would be immediately drafted into the army. The sociology department didn't know what to do. Failing these students at the exam board would mean almost certainly that a proportion of them would end up in body bags. Morrie decided to give all his male students A grades regardless. No one dropped out, and the US army was denied an influx of young sociologists.

Teaching had been Morrie's life. So he set out to teach one more class in the face of death. It would be conducted as a personal tutorial with his old student who had returned to him from his life as a successful sports journalist. The lessons would take place on Tuesdays, like virtually all of the courses he had taught before. This book is not about a dying man; it is about how to live. I think it's almost impossible not to love it. Some readers whom I forced it upon have suggested that the book sails too close to sentimentality. True, I sometimes yearned for Morrie to do something mean to make him a more familiar human compound of virtue and failing. But the book is not ultimately sentimental – rather, it carries real sentiment.

No doubt there were some of Morrie's students who were impatient with his eccentric antics and educational experiments. I can imagine that Morrie would have his detractors in today's universities where students want value for money and lecturers are expected to impart their knowledge in easily digestible forms through podcasts, PowerPoint slides and the like. But beyond all this, Morrie's story also underlines what is at stake in higher education. Albom's lean and moving book reads like an extended epitaph. Towards the end Morrie expressed regret for the books he might have written but hadn't. These are sobering passages in the contemporary climate where the injunction to write looms large over academic departments.

As universities become more businesslike and we end up viewing our students as, at best, paying customers, or, at worst, distractions that keep us from the real work of writing and research, it is easy to forget that universities are also places where teachers can play a small role in helping students, not just through the curriculum, but in life itself. This is, of course, not a one-way process and I am often struck by how much I learn in supervisions and seminars. I am not sure 'who is teaching who' half the time. *Tuesdays with Morrie* is a reminder that sometimes things of enduring consequence happen for those on both sides of the lectern in the lecture hall.

In some quarters it has become fashionable to speak of ghosts and 'the dead' in a clever or supercilious fashion. The great Peruvian poet César Vallejo once wrote that 'nothing is possible in death, except on top of what is left in life'. I think the written word is often an attempt to leave such traces. George Orwell claimed that one of the reasons he wrote was 'to be remembered'. What I find compelling about Morrie's story is that he chose to make his mark through teaching. The beautiful irony is that his student turned scribe and page by page transposed his spectral voice. And this, I think, is the miracle at the heart of this book.

Campus Watch

'The first casualty when war comes is truth,' remarked US Senator Hiram Warren Johnson in 1918. The Republican from California was liberal on social issues but remained a strong advocate of American isolationism and questioned US involvement in world affairs. He died on 6 August 1945, on the day that the atomic bomb was dropped on Hiroshima. With wars in Afghanistan and Iraq and the threat of further confrontations in the Middle East, might the search for knowledge become another type of collateral damage?

Orwell wrote in his dystopian classic *Nineteen Eighty-Four* that ceaseless combat at a distance 'helps to preserve the special mental atmosphere'. In the United States since 11 September 2001 US foreign policy has created an atmosphere of intolerance with regard to views that are deemed unpatriotic, particularly on campus. Middle East studies has been the first area to really feel the effect of anxieties about homeland security.

In late September 2002 an organization called Campus Watch (http://www.campus-watch.org/) was set up with its own website. Its mission is to provide 'reviews and critiques of Middle East studies in North America with an aim to improving

128

them. The project mainly addresses five problems: analytical failures, the mixing of politics with scholarship, intolerance of alternative views, apologetics, and the abuse of power over students.' As of February 2014 the website contains reports on sixty-seven campuses, identifying academics who express views against the interests of government foreign policy or which address the organization's five key problems.

Miriam Cooke, Professor of Modern Arab Literature at Duke University, was the target of Campus Watch's ire. A talk she gave at Duke's John Hope Franklin Center on 26 March 2003 was reported under the headline 'Duke Feminist Gives Thumbs Up to Taliban'. The correspondent wrote:

> Cooke rejected the liberation of Afghan women as a reason to go to war. Rather than being grateful for calling attention to the suffering of fellow women, she castigated First Lady Laura Bush . . . Cooke accused Laura Bush of furthering 'the imperial project in her highly gendered appeal to a world conscience'.

On close scrutiny, it is clear that the story was compiled from a series of sources available online indicating that it was more than just a disgruntled response to one talk. 'Initially, I was surprised because the report was accurate,' says Cooke, laughing. 'I remember thinking "That is what I think!" But then I got lots of hateful emails and partly what was shocking was the speed with which they gathered all those responses.'

For Cooke, the current climate where academics are expected to act in the national interest raises a series of difficult questions. 'How can Middle East specialists continue to research and write responsibly without being caught in the "patriotism" trap? How can we critique tyrants like Saddam Hussein without falling into the arms of Campus Watch advocates and thereby working towards the perpetuation of greater injustice?' she asks.

Students inform on their teachers in the name of self-protection: 'un-American' faculty members are accused of abusing their power. It seems from reading these accounts that any criticism of US foreign policy is aligned with tacit support for the Taliban or al Qaeda. Some view this as a 'special problem' for Middle East studies but others suggest this indicates an overall shift in the mental atmosphere in US academic life.

Judith Butler, Professor of Rhetoric and Comparative Literature at Berkeley, wrote:

> To charge those who voice critical views with treason, terrorist sympathizing, anti-Semitism, moral relativism, postmodernism, juvenile behaviour, collaboration, anachronistic Leftism, is to seek to destroy the credibility not of the views that are held, but of the persons who hold them. It produces a climate of fear in which to voice a certain view is to risk being branded and shamed with a heinous appellation.

Universities are precious because they afford the opportunity to take risks in thinking to develop an understanding beyond parochial self-assurance.

Returning to Senator Warren's famous comment, perhaps it is doubt – and not truth – that is the first casualty of war. The captains of war in our time suffer not from doubt but rather from certainty, a kind of simplistic confidence in a bid to compensate for unprecedented risks and evident global vulnerability. No one ever pulled a trigger, dropped a bomb or informed on a teacher in a state of doubt. It seems the invitation to academic thinking is to question and reach beyond the false comforts of cosy homeland views.

The 'mental atmosphere' in the United States is certainly different to what we recognize in the United Kingdom but I think the real risk is that there is a convergence happening.

In February 2015 Home Secretary Theresa May announced, as part of the government's Counter-terrorism and Security bill, plans that make it a legal duty for academics to prevent students from being drawn into terrorism. This would also require academics to vet the content of lectures by visiting speakers and also to scrutinize and ultimately report on student behaviour.

A letter protesting these proposals was signed by 500 professors including Sir John Ball, the Oxford mathematician, Sir Tom Kibble, co-discoverer of the Higgs mechanism and Higgs boson, emeritus Goldsmiths Professor Pat Caplan and Professor Paul Gilroy, author of the classic study *Ain't No Black in the Union Jack*.

The signatories make a powerful argument for the value of open debate and the folly of closing down campus debate through fostering a climate of fear. They wrote:

The best response to acts of terror against UK civilians is to maintain and defend an open, democratic society in which discriminatory behaviour of any kind is effectively challenged. Ensuring colleges and universities can continue to debate difficult and unpopular issues is a vital part of this. Draconian crackdowns on the rights of academics and students will not achieve the ends the government says it seeks.

It is a reminder though that the value of the university is, in part, to offer an opportunity to see the issues of the day outside of the confines of national interest. Knowledge cannot be policed by the boundaries of the state or its geopolitical priorities. Part of what universities are needed for today is to foster a critical imagination that is truly global and cosmopolitan in reach, that lives with doubt in the service of understanding.

Writing Routines and the Torture of Starting

Writing is just difficult, plain and simple. The temptation to put off writing is strong as a result. We end up becoming what psychologist Paul J. Silvia calls 'binge writers'. Delaying the moment when we sit down to write means we are then faced with a deadline that can only be met through late-night binges at the keyboard. For Silvia the only way out of this pattern is to become a routine writer and treat writing time as a non-negotiable commitment, like teaching a class or attending a department board meeting. His little book entitled *How to Write a Lot* (2007) is crammed with useful tips on how to foster better literary habits.

We all have periods in the day when we are most intellectually awake, which is when we should be writing. I try and write in the mornings because that is when my mind is most agile. Sometimes, like this morning, I wake up at 4.30 a.m. and suddenly a link or a connection I was trying to make in something I am working on becomes clear. I find that I have no real control over that process because ideas can't simply be willed to come. Leonard Cohen commented once that he didn't know where the good songs came from because if he did he'd visit that place more often.

Imaginative leaps or analytical connections are like that too. They seem to me like unexpected guests that we need to be ready to receive at any time. For some reason my daily cycle to work is often a moment when a turn of phrase or idea comes into focus. I know I have been spotted on more than one occasion recording the arrival of an idea at the roadside with a few scribbles in my notebook dressed in full cycling regalia.

Having said this, I do give myself designated periods of time to write. The torture for me is starting. Once I've started I am usually fine but if I get interrupted – if the phone rings, or if something else intervenes and time drifts – then I am really in trouble. I usually give myself a block of time rather than whole days. I find that after three to four hours of writing intensely I start to achieve less and less.

The other thing that I try to do is stop a writing session before I have exhausted all of the things I wanted to say. Always leave an argument or description to be written. So, I never stop writing without knowing what the next point is going to be. It makes picking up the thread the next time easier.

That Special Pen

I have always had a weakness for a nice pen. They don't have to be expensive ones to qualify: a fibre tip Pentel or a smooth writing gel roller nib will do just fine. It is something about the smoothness of how they write and the flow of the ink as it moves over the paper. Whenever I visit a university overseas I always make sure to go hunting in the college shop for an exotic pen. It is only recently that I have come to appreciate quite how widespread this kind of stationery fetishism is among writers and academics. Maybe it shouldn't be surprising that as writers we fetishize the main tool of our trade. After all, pens are the tongue of the mind, as Cervantes once put it.

There is a beautiful picture of Simone De Beauvoir sitting in Café de Flore, Paris holding her Esterbrook fountain pen over a blank sheet of paper. It is a wonderful portrait of an intellectual at work. A stylish pen is not compulsory and many great thinkers used more humble writing implements. For example, Stuart Hall wrote with green Pentel R50 ball pens producing thick lines that made his scratchy handwriting barely legible. When George Orwell was too sick with tuberculosis to use a typewriter David Astor supplied him with biros – which were a recent invention in the late forties – so that he could continue to work, although tellingly, Orwell's protagonist in *Nineteen Eighty-Four*, Winston Smith, chooses a nib ink-pen instead of an 'ink-pencil' to write his seditious secret diary. This 'archaic instrument' provides a weapon to strike back at doublethink. With this pen he printed the fateful words 'DOWN WITH BIG BROTHER'.

The love of pens is often linked with the aesthetic virtues of handwriting. For Mary Gordon it is the very physicality of writing that is valuable because 'it involves flesh, blood and the thingness of pen and paper'. The physical act of writing this way for Gordon is a way of grounding her imagination in the world of objects and flesh. Anthropologist Tim Ingold is an avid exponent of writing by hand. For him writing on a computer is 'joyless and soul-destroying' and 'rips the heart out of writing'. For Ingold handwriting with a fountain pen is similar to making true notes on a musical instrument. He writes: 'I compare it to practising my cello. When I practise – which I do as often as I can – the sound pours out from the contact between bow and strings. In just the same way, handwriting flows from the moving point of contact between pen and paper.' He argues that writing on a keyboard by contrast ruptures the connection between lines, movement and words.

Roland Barthes was another enthusiast for writing by hand. In an interview first published in 1973, he confessed that he had an 'almost obsessive relation to writing instruments'. Like Ingold, he favoured a fountain pen for its capacity to produce 'soft, smooth writing'. However, Barthes makes a distinction between two different kinds of graphic impulses. The first he calls the production of a 'calligraphic object'. This is the initial stage of drafting longhand with a pen. The second stage he called the creation of a 'typographical object', which is typed and a text created for 'anonymous and collective consumption'. Barthes' writing process consisted of a first draft written by hand which would then in turn be typed and re-drafted.

That Special Pen

Without being conscious of it I realize now I have followed Barthes' methods too. I write first by hand, often in notebooks, and then re-type later once the ideas have some initial form. Longhand allows for the freedom to sketch thoughts in the way that Ingold suggests. Also, the slowness of writing this way gives the pen in my hand enough time to catch up with the thoughts in my head. There is something about the tension between the two that helps to consolidate and give shape to the ideas scribbled on the pages of my notebook.

For many years the loss of a 'special pen' caused little concern because they were replaceable. As time has passed those cheap disposable pens have been replaced. Stephen Dobson, an old friend who I met while a student at Goldsmiths, gave me an expensive Mont Blanc fountain pen – like the one Georges Perec used – for my 40th birthday. Then a decade later I received a beautiful silver Cross fountain pen from another friend and colleague, Michael Keith. These truly special pens have none of the disposable qualities of their plastic predecessors.

Now, misplacing either of them causes a deep sense of panic. I can't think about anything else and in the midst of a frantic search I can feel myself breaking out into a cold sweat. I don't take the Mont Blanc pen out of the house now for fear of losing it. This problem has reached such a pitch that I can feel the collective shudder of dread in my family when I shout down the stairs, 'Has anyone seen my silver pen?!'

Earlier in the year I was preparing a lecture for a conference in Tokyo. The event also coincided with the publication of a Japanese translation of one of my books: it was a big deal. I needed to send the manuscript of the lecture ahead of the trip. As usual I had sketched out my talk in a notebook in longhand with my special silver Cross pen. All was in hand.

The next morning I went to my bag to look for the silver pen to scribble another note but it was not there. I asked everyone in the family and they had not seen it. I searched the house frantically to no avail. The pen was nowhere to be found. I retraced my steps. Could I have left it in my office? Did I leave it on the train? I was getting myself into such a fog of panic that I couldn't think about anything else.

This went on for several days and now time was running out. I needed to turn the handwritten draft of the lecture into what Barthes would call a 'typographical object' but all I could think about was the whereabouts of my lost pen. Then I started to get angry with myself. 'What is the matter with me?!' Here I was facing a serious deadline for an international event that I couldn't afford to screw up but all I could think about was this infernal pen. My family were sick of hearing me go on about it. I had lost almost an entire week. I wasn't going to write my talk with the bloody pen anyway! Pull yourself together.

I gave myself a mental pep talk as I cycled to work the following day with a laptop safely installed in my backpack. 'Just concentrate on re-drafting the lecture,' I kept thinking. If the silver pen is lost then there is nothing I can do about it. I felt a sense of calm resignation at last taking hold as I ped-dled through Hilly Fields Park, close to Goldsmiths. There is a café there called Pistachios and I often use it as a writing refuge. 'Maybe I'll stop off and have a coffee and get started with re-drafting the lecture? Good plan,' I thought.

I peeled off my cycling gear and put my laptop down, stak-ing a claim to a table. The café is always a calming place. I love working there, a place to be undisturbed and think, even when it is crowded. I chat to Sheryl who is originally from Australia as she makes my coffee. Unable to free my-self from my pen anxiety, I ask half-heartedly: 'You haven't had a silver pen handed in by any chance, have you?' Sheryl holds up her finger: 'Hold on a minute.' She goes to the box of abandoned things under the counter and emerges with a shiny writing implement. 'Do you mean this one?' she says.

That Special Pen

There it was. Fred, the owner, came over and said, 'Oh that's a shame, I had my eye on that nice pen myself!'

The euphoria on being reunited with my beloved Cross pen is a combination of utter relief and the sigh of deep inner calm. Later, I realize the pen is no longer just a special writing tool but rather it has become a kind of existential compass. I don't quite understand its mysterious secret powers and I am no longer sure whether I control it or it controls me.

Perhaps the silver Cross pen has become a symbol of the curse of writing itself. Mary Gordon commented: 'There are maybe some writers who contemplate a day's work without dread, but I don't know them . . . It's a bad business, this writing . . . We accomplish what we do, creating a series of stratagems to explore the horror.' I have become a hostage to the routines and tricks that keep me to the task and this includes handwriting with a particular pen. The anxiety felt when that special pen goes missing is the price I pay for those otherwise comforting writing rituals.

Viral Warning

Anyone on campus over 30 is likely to think that the word 'viral' refers to some kind of nasty affliction. Our students will know that 'viral emails' are a twenty-first-century cultural phenomenon including anything from animated political satires to spoof clips, hilarious bloopers and pornographic jokes. They are viewed, laughed at and passed on, creating a vast global online comedy club.

In 2006 the Institute of Contemporary Arts in London put on the world's first exhibition of virals entitled 'Outrageous and Contagious'. The show offered a peep into the kind of content likely to be hiding in our students' inboxes. The exhibition was a collaboration between Channel 4's Ideas Factory, BoreMe.com and the digital agency Ralph and viral promoter Hot Cherry. The organizers maintain that virals represent a democratization of creativity. Through using relatively cheap digital tools like mobile videophones, Photoshop, digital video recorders and iMovie home editing software almost anyone can make a film or cartoon. Like any joke, the acid test of a viral is simply whether or not it is funny.

One of my favourites was a spoof ad that showed a garish portrait of Christ with a beaming smile on his face with the caption 'IT'S A MIRACLE' across his chest. Beneath his unperforated palms were tubes of the UniBond adhesive No More Nails. The poet E.E. Cummings said the most wasted of all days is one without laugher. Loud eruptions of mirth provided the exhibition's soundtrack as individuals crowded around the PCs in a room that was ill-equipped to deal with the level of interest. The hundreds of people who queued through the corridors of the ICA to view the exhibition were not squandering the Bank Holiday.

Virals are coming to the curriculum too as universities are starting to use them as 'live briefs' on communication and design courses. They may prove difficult to contain academically if the content of BoreMe.com is anything to go by. We are accustomed to students using their mobiles to text each other during lectures but we might also have to cope with irrepressible laughter. If they are not receiving them already, students will soon be able to have their favourite virals delivered directly to their mobiles. That's not all.

A group of American viral makers going under the name of Prangstgrüp chose a lecture given by a chemistry professor at Columbia as the location for their 'viral shoot'. His innocent invitation for further questions is met by a student who stands up and shouts, 'Hey teach – I gotta question.' The academic hush is broken. From somewhere in the auditorium the rhythm of an orchestral arrangement strikes up in the style of a Broadway show. The protagonist launches into song: 'We come to class each day/ It seems we all fall asleep/ We've lost our dreams.' The undergraduate, Jean Valjean, leads a full cast of accomplices through a routine that would rival any stage production. The hapless professor can do no more than laugh it off and join in the final applause.

Mark Twain said 'the only really effective weapon is laughter' and a viral spoof might just be playing in a lecture hall near you very soon.

10 April

Ivory Towers

In the 2002 academic year much ink was spilt over the now notorious outburst of Geoffrey Sampson, Professor of Natural Language Computing at the University of Sussex, who claimed in a paper published on his website that 'racialism' is inevitable and universal. 'Yellow-skinned Orientals tend to be brighter than whites and Negroes tend to be rather less bright' wrote Sampson. In the *Times Higher Education Supplement* Ian McDonald observed, 'Outside the academy, Sampson's article represents little more than a footnote in the outpouring of racist myths and lies of the past few years. But, unchallenged, its potential power lies in the rationalization of an intuitive sense that many people will hold, namely that preference for racial familiarity is "natural".'

In the aftermath of McDonald's article a debate was hosted on the (then) *THES* website. It made for telling reading. A host of liberal-minded academics lined up, shoulder to shoulder with right-wing libertarians and pernicious racists, to defend Sampson's academic freedom. By turns, 'racist academics' were accused of 'lacking confidence' in their own arguments, 'political correctness' and of not being 'tough enough to defend principles'. In short, those who were offended by

Sampson's outpouring were accused of being too 'thin-skinned', not being able to take the 'raciological' knocks.

Such forms of counterblast are launched from within the armature of an assumed whiteness – perhaps even invisible to those protected by it – that staked out the terms of the argument. Ben Carrington concluded that those involved in the online debate had 'virtually nothing to say about racism and how it might be challenged'. For him, this whole incident 're-veals just how deeply entrenched racism, in its various guises, still is within the HE sector'.

Racism in higher education can take a very crude and brutal form. It furnishes assumptions that black staff will take care of the 'race dimensions' of the curriculum, or that black or Asian colleagues will automatically be 'good with the ethnics'. In another sense, whiteness works like an implicit authorization of what is valued and taken to be 'cutting-edge work'. Perhaps one way forward is to try and identify the kinds of 'cultural passports' that are necessary to gain entry to the academy. These boundaries are policed through the implicit knowledge necessary to acquire academic forms of distinction. It seems to me that some of what we might call institutional racism is unwritten, embedded and embodied within the academy's sheer institutional weight.

Most white academics see it as unthinkable and unreasonable that any accusation of racism should be levelled at their door. For them, the face of racism is that of the moral degenerate, the hateful bigot, or the mad/eccentric. Couched in these terms it becomes unthinkable that such an ugly word could be directed at genteel, educated and liberal dons. Even raising the issue of institutional racism tentatively in HE produces responses such as 'How could you?' or 'How dare you make such accusations?' Rather than simply hide in the refusal to acknowledge the problem – that is, the rebuff 'Don't look at me!' – the open question that whites needs to embrace is 'Why not me?'

I am not suggesting that the addiction to white supremacy should be countered by some kind of equivalent to an AA meeting – 'Hi. My name's Les. I am a recovering white person.' No, rather it needs to be acknowledged that racism has done damage to reason, done damage to academic and civic freedoms, and has done damage to the project of education itself. Admitting this means a kind of resolute and ongoing reckoning with whiteness. It is never a matter of an end point, or a smug achievement, be it the form of a rewritten university mission statement or the adoption of a race equality policy.

Rather, it is an ongoing questioning that strives to step out of whiteness's brilliant shadow. The kind of reflexivity I am arguing for should be troublesome and uncomfortable because, as John Dewey pointed out, it is a matter of embracing a 'willingness to endure a condition of mental unrest and disturbance'. This is driven not by guilt but by shame. It is shameful to read in research published by the University of Leeds that black colleagues in British universities are routinely undermined, cut out of the loop of academic communication and subjected to crude racism inside and outside the classroom.

Many who have felt the velvet glove of academic exclusion in the job market are reluctant to speak out because of fear of ostracism or being labelled a 'troublemaker'. Racism in HE can't be pushed under the carpet any longer; too much has been deposited there already and there are too many undulations along the faculty floor. If the sheer weight of whiteness that bears down on the academy is to be lifted, there needs to be an open and difficult acknowledgement of the damage that racism has done inside the education system. Then, and perhaps only then, will universities be ready to play a role in producing a post-imperial society that is at peace with itself.

Conference Etiquette

The temporary academic relocations of conference season take us not only to strange and sometimes remote campuses but also suspend usual routines of behaviour. A friend and colleague said recently that there are distinct national types of conference etiquette. How would she characterize them? 'Australian conferences are vicious and boozy, American conferences are status conscious and networking-obsessed and British conferences are polite and consensual.' The insight in the observation triggered immediate flashbacks. In continental Europe it is different again, where conference participants don't ask questions but rather 'intervene'. It is hearsay but it is rumoured that on one occasion a prestigious French academic asked a question that lasted 45 minutes.

American conferences are conducted within an atmosphere of pragmatic professionalism, business cards are traded, dinner invitations jockeyed for and conversations between delegates sound like curriculum vitae being read aloud. There is also something very peculiar in the staged formality of US conference discussion that reveals their obsession with status. Even the closest of friends refer to each other with their full academic titles to emphasize to the audience rank and esteem:

'I would like to respond to a point made by Professor War-
show [my long-time friend and former lover] . . . concerning
one key aspect of this quite brilliant paper.'

Conferences are places of self-promotion. 'Hold that book
up higher,' says the keynote speaker to the poor soul chairing,
as her latest literary offering is hoisted skyward like a football
trophy. It all seems to have become much more brazen in the
colloquium marketplace. Like barrow boys flogging bunches of bananas, publications are advertised on the PowerPoint
slides as if to set out the stall of ideas. 'Get your journal article
citations here, three for a pound!' Sycophancy is the other tool
at work here. It can be transparent but nonetheless effective.
Even the most acerbic of critics finds it hard to resist being
seduced by a compliment.

While there is plenty of this going on in Britain, conference
etiquette in my colleague's diagnosis is quite different. The
choreography of thanks to the organizers, co-panellists and indeed all those who have assembled at some ridiculous hour is
terribly polite. Audiences nod like the purple cows that dec-
orated the back seat windows of Ford Cortinas in the 1970s.
Questions are introduced with the prefix 'Thanks, I really enjoyed your paper but . . .' Aching reverence is the preferred
mode of self-presentation. In a plenary session a sociologist
chastised the delegates at the event for too much nodding:
'Aren't the nods of agreement all a bit too cosy? Shouldn't
more people be shaking their heads instead?' As silent encour-
agement to a speaker the nod shows attentiveness and appreciation. I myself am a Pavlovian nodder; it is the condition-
al reflex inspired through attending too many conferences.
Yet as Pierre Bourdieu might say, truth isn't measured in nods
of approval.

There is a sinister aspect poking up through this surface
of gentility. As a colleague put it, it's 'a very British way of
telling someone their whole project is worthless without tell-

ing them'. It does not quite name itself but is nonetheless conveyed. 'Thanks very much for your paper...' followed by a list
of shortcomings that lead inexorably to the conclusion that it
is ill-founded and actually not worth the effort or the paper it
is written on. This is a very British, controlled viciousness that
can be damning while at the same time very well mannered.

There are a few maverick exceptions that luxuriate in
breaking this stifling politeness. These modes of barbed response – most often masculine in character – either take the
form of bad-tempered intellectual tantrums ('I just have to say
that you are all fundamentally wrong') or the reproachful ser-
mons from those who see themselves as the Defenders of the
Discipline and its founding Great Men. In the latter case, such
intellectual knights play to the conference gallery which is either enchanted or merely entertained by such charismatic cer-
tainties and yet they often define their discipline in such tight
and exclusive ways that membership of this club is limited to
themselves.

In 2009 conference etiquette was rudely interrupted by
Russian artist Alexander Brener who staged his forms of extreme curating at academic events at Goldsmiths. The rumour
around the college was that during a cultural studies seminar
on 'The Knowledge Economy and the Future of Capitalism',
he dropped his trousers, defecated in a cup, placed it on the
table where the speakers were sitting and said, quoting Agamben, 'There – that's "bare life!"' It was said that murmurs went
around the room, 'call the police' but this was quickly ruled
out – 'you can't call the police to a cultural studies seminar'.
Then, re-establishing the decorum of conference etiquette,
those assembled just carried on regardless. Actually, it turned
out later that this stunt was less than a live event and in fact
had been pre-prepared.

Soon after, at another event at which I was present, one
of Brener's associates piped up at the end of a long technical

philosophical discussion between Andrew Benjamin and Scott Lash on Agamben's *The Time That Remains*. 'You are all quite wrong about what Agamben meant,' she said scolding the philosophers and theory students. 'I know this,' she continued, 'because he was my lover . . .'

Perhaps such pranks could only happen in the art school environment of Goldsmiths but even then the scatological shock value soon becomes cliché. The lesson here is that we should think more about presenting our ideas and research as forms of performance and this is not just a matter of being more theatrical.

Rather, it makes us think about how we convey our ideas and use our voices. I remember organizing a conference where an experienced and eminent academic gave a presentation where the large audience that had gathered could barely hear what she had to say. This was because she pointed the microphone towards the audience rather than holding it close to her mouth. One of the attendees from a London-based theatre group came up to speak to me after the session. She attended the event because her company was developing an idea for a production on the theme of the conference. After the session she asked gently: 'Do academics get any voice training?' It was a telling question because we don't really think about our voices as our most fundamental medium of communication.

I know when I am nervous I have an unfortunate habit of putting my index finger on my top lip. It was only after seeing myself lecture on YouTube that I realized I did this unconsciously. The problem is when I do this my voice is reduced to a mumble and disappears like I am whispering a secret to myself. While watching myself on YouTube was a painful experience, I learned a lot about the things I needed to change about how I might communicate better. It's worth trying, even though watching yourself present on screen is perhaps the most cringingly awkward thing you'll ever do.

147

Conference Etiquette

In my time as Dean of the Goldsmiths Graduate School I saw students experimenting with really imaginative ways of performing ideas.

The best example I can think of is Heidi Hasbrouck's ethnography of female waitresses in American diners and restaurants. Heidi was presenting her research at the Goldsmiths Graduate Festival. As the audience filed in, they smelt coffee being made and set up on a table at the side of the lecture theatre. Heidi, dressed in her waitress uniform, greeted the conference delegates. 'Can I get you a coffee? Cream? Sugar?' The audience was mildly confused while accepting a gratefully received dose of harsh-tasting coffee.

As we settled to listen to Heidi give her paper – still in costume – we realized that she had been embodying her argument. Central to this kind of work is a gendered form of emotional labour. Part of what a waitress does is the performance of a gendered cultural script. This involves tending to the patrons' needs but also making them feel attended to and cared for. Heidi inhabited her argument before she explicated it.

Giving a conference paper requires putting one's ideas forward and by extension putting oneself in peril. Will I seem a fool? Will I be found out? It involves a kind of existential risk evident in the nervous way that speakers ask, 'How do you think it went?' I keep trying to stop myself asking this but it is impossible. The sense of exposure breeds uncertainty that can keep you awake at night and haunt you for days afterwards. What did they mean by that question? What was behind the pained expression of the person in the third row? In the context of this private form of academic torture British conference etiquette – and even a bit of nodding – is merciful. The fact is people rarely tell the truth when asked for an assessment on how the paper went and secretly we really always know the answer anyway.

148

Academic Rights

About ten years ago a letter dropped through my letterbox from the Authors' Licensing & Collecting Society (ALCS). It said they were holding royalties for me and on becoming a member the payment would be transferred. My first reaction was that this was just another junk mail con trick. I am sure you've all received letters that start with 'Congratulations – you've just won £50,000.' It was only after speaking to a friend who had received royalties from ALCS that I dug the letter out of the recycling bin and made further inquiries.

ALCS is a non-profit-making company that distributes payments to authors for the reproduction of their work. With over 80,000 members it is one of the largest writers' organizations in the world. In 2013/14 ALCS announced a record with £33,755,233 of incomes to be distributed to its members. In large part the revenue is generated by licences given to photocopy an already published work but it also covers digitization of printed texts and broadcasting and cable re-transmission.

This year I received payments from sources as obscure as a Scandinavian anthropology department that photocopied a chapter I'd written for an edited book and the re-broadcast in Russia of a radio interview I'd done for the BBC. The scale of the uncollected royalties held by ALCS is quite staggering. The Copyright Licensing Agency, the body that issues licences to photocopy material, transfers the author's share automatically to ALCS. The society is entrusted to seek out the authors and pass on the payments.

ALCS holds literally millions of pounds in unpaid royalties and this is just the figure for writers that ALCS has tracked down but who haven't returned their registration forms. Usually authors of books automatically keep the copyright for their work and publishers insist on exclusive publication rights. This means that while publishers can protect their interests, authors have ownership of their work and get paid for further reproduction. It is quite another matter when it comes to academic journals. Publishers often insist that authors transfer copyright for their journal articles to the publisher.

Under pressure to publish in a climate dominated by the research assessments and an increasingly competitive job market, academic writers – particularly young ones – simply publish at any cost, even if it means signing away the rights to their work. In truth, academic writers are often in too weak a position to bargain. We simply sacrifice the rights to our work as the price to be paid for making it into the pages of a prestigious journal. Taylor & Francis, which publishes more than 700 journals, requests that authors transfer their rights because it is 'standard practice in serial and journals publishing'. Its rationale, posted on its website, is that publisher ownership of copyright gives 'protection against infringement, libel and plagiarism'.

Additionally, it suggests that publisher control enables an efficient response to 'requests from third parties to reproduce, reprint, or translate an article' in accordance with international copyright law, so 'encouraging the dissemination of knowledge'. Every academic would welcome the 'dissemination of knowledge' but such platitudes mask other interests. The result is that the publisher benefits from any extra revenue produced from reproduction or re-use; the author is entitled to nothing.

Unlike commercial publishing, the scientific, technical and medical market (STM) is low risk and stable. The Anglo-Dutch publishing giant Reed Elsevier is the global market leader for STM publications with 1,700 primary research and review journals. Its best known textbook is Gray's Anatomy and the company specializes in medicine, nursing and education journals and reference texts. The company's annual turnover is over £5 billion. At first glance the academic sector seems like a financial graveyard. Yet, on closer inspection there are considerable financial benefits. *The Huffington Post* commented in 2014 that academic journals were 'the most profitable obsolete technology in history'. They quoted a study that pointed out that in 2013 Elsevier posted higher profits (39%) than technology giant Apple (37%). The prices for academic journals can remain relatively high because university libraries are willing to pay for essential journals in perpetuity.

Similarly, key professional textbooks in the fields of medicine and law can hold a high price because they contain 'must-have information' and students simply have to buy them. This is why publishers are increasingly pressing academic authors to write textbooks. Meanwhile, we are all clamouring to publish original work in journals with high 'impact factors' because of the Research Excellence Framework and this fits well with the publishing status quo. Editorial boards are swamped with submissions and publishers not only get the copy for free but they may also benefit from owning its copyright.

The truth is, academics don't expect to get paid for their writing. Indeed, I am not sure that we even see ourselves as writers in the broader sense of the term. We are expected to pore over the keyboard for love, enlightenment or something less profane than cold cash. Yet academic publishing is inherently unfair. Academic authors are not just expected to write for nothing, we are also subsidizing the profits of publishers by doing so. We have to find ways of placing pressure on publishers to change. Perhaps this can only start when we try harder to hold onto the copyright for our work. Otherwise we will be condemned to mine away with little pay or recompense at the frontiers of knowledge.

Casts of Mind

Orientation to the human condition within the academic cast of mind can be characterized on a spectrum. At one end there are writers whose subjects appear like heroic characters in a John Steinbeck novel. These profane angels are always the bearers of goodness and purity of intention regardless of what the evils of society present them with. Nothing messy is admitted and all the shadowy corners in human experience are edited out as are their inevitable human moral failings. It strikes me, reading accounts of human life produced by these well-intentioned cheerleaders, that they actually make their protected subjects less than human. I know that I have been guilty of this in my own writing.

At the other end of the spectrum there are commentators who relish the foibles and weaknesses of the all too human objects of their discourse. For this group the story of human fallibility is what makes life worth living. They are the Philip Roths of scholastic commentary, which is not at all limited to what they write about: they take wicked pleasure in tales of the honours student who falls foul of the law or the faculty member caught in some incriminating activity. Failings are to be savoured and shared like a non-alimentary course at a dinner party.

Casts of Mind

As Spinoza wrote, our task is 'not to deride, bewail, or execrate human actions, but to understand'. This involves neither piety nor censorship and the admission that none of us is so perfect. This 'moral low ground' would accept imperfection as an instrument to comprehend human action.

Few academics in my experience are equal to the ancient Greek aphorism 'Know yourself'. Rather we are strangers to ourselves. Theodor Adorno commented that 'the splinter in your eye is the best magnifying glass'. Here this can take on another kind of meaning. That the inspection of the moral failings of others should induce, like Adorno's splinter, a discomfort regarding the shape of our own flaws and maybe that would make gleeful derision less comfy.

The Devil You Know

Rejection is a professional hazard in academic life. It can take the form of a cast out grant application, or a 'thanks but no thanks' missive from an academic journal or publisher. Part of the challenge of becoming an academic writer is how to avoid being defeated by failure. Samuel Beckett might well have been referring to the academy when he wrote in his prose piece 'Worstward Ho': 'Ever tried. Ever failed. No matter. Try again. Fail again. Fail better.'

But the price of academic failure is increasing. In the UK, funding of university departments is in large part determined through the assessment of staff research and publications. So getting published and raising research money is increasingly essential in the hothouse of higher education. Yet the fate of proposals and written work is in large part sealed by people whose names we do not know. They are the anonymous referees whom funding agencies and editorial boards summon to pass expert judgement.

Ros Gill has argued that the reviewing process is becoming increasingly toxic and cruel. Citing a number of examples she shows how 'critical evaluation' is reduced to destructive, dismissive and undermining personal attacks. Every academic has a collection of reviews of this kind. Gill suggests that the reviewer's ire is fed by the competitiveness and frustrations of contemporary academic culture. Here, she argues, the person under review becomes the target of a 'repressed rage bursting out as an attack against someone who is not the cause of it . . . where academics may feel that they can exercise some power – thus they "let rip", occasionally cruelly, under the cloak of guaranteed anonymity'.

In a world where debates over freedom of information and civil rights are increasingly being connected, can we defend a situation where the fruits of our intellectual labours are decided by nameless judges who are not held accountable for the content of their opinions? I know many people, myself included, who have pored over a referee's comments for lexical fingerprints, those telltale traces of the reviewer's identity such as references to their own written output, evidence of their pet concerns or penchant for archaic printer fonts. Negative reviews which damn with faint praise are particularly devastating for a research grant application. With competition for research council grants so high, it only takes one negative review to consign an application to the dustbin.

Defenders of retaining the anonymous reviewing system argue that it allows reviewers to be frank and honest. 'If reviewers had to be named it would lead to anodyne and meaninglessly bland assessments,' they say. Or, more self-interestedly: 'If colleagues knew I had written their review they would never invite me to give conference papers, or to contribute to edited books.' But isn't concealment the worst kind of deceit? 'I'd be delighted to go to Rome on an academic freebie, so long as I can keep under wraps that I sabotaged your publishing aspirations.' These are weak justifications.

Often editorial boards have to act as the arbiters in this play of personal grudges and tainted judgement. Editors are in the unenviable position of having to decide how much of the brutal detail in the referee's report to disclose. The best try to protect the sometimes fragile confidence of scholars by filtering out their worst excesses. These difficult editorial dilemmas might easily be avoided if the system were more transparent.

Anonymity has provided a mask behind which petty jealousies, envy, spitefulness, rivalry and intellectual sectarianism has flourished. This can also operate with devastating effect within the research assessment exercises like the Research Excellence Framework that operates within an anonymous peer review system. Hiding behind anonymity, reviewers can savage the work of a whole department while at the same time recruit some of the very same colleagues to be included in their own edited collections.

My strength of feeling on this issue was sealed when a senior professor of sociology sent me his comments on an article I'd written with John Solomos and Tim Crabbe that he'd refereed. In a scribbled note he explained that he 'didn't believe in anonymous reviewing'. It has to be said that his comments were fairly trenchant, but I respected him all the more because he did not hide behind the referee's privilege of secrecy. He made me realize that anonymous reviewing is a bankrupt and indefensible practice.

Now when I write a review of applications or a paper I follow his example, and send my comments directly to its author(s), and I would encourage others to do so. I've heard it said this would make it harder to find reviewers, particularly for journal submissions.

But I think we have to have more backbone. Such transparency might even make reviewing more careful and thoughtful. This problem doesn't end with deciding the fate of grant applications and journal submissions; the lack of accountability in criticism is a symptom of a wider syndrome. Our intellectual culture is sadly lacking an ethics of measured critique. Cheap and vituperative asides creep into the best academic writing.

As a result, argument can degenerate all too quickly into name-calling. Years of scholarly endeavour can be dismissed with a few cutting sentences aimed only to bolster their author's credentials and authenticity. This has produced a situation in which appearing to be a harsh critic – and in teaching the equivalent is being a tough marker – is a prized attribute and evidence of a truly 'pumped up' brain. This is little more than a form of intellectual machismo – which can be embraced equally by women and men – so that substantive disagreement becomes almost a sideshow. My view is simple. If the critics do not have the integrity to be accountable for the content of their assessments, they shouldn't put fingers to keyboard.

Supervision

Today a PhD student came to see me after a quite long hiatus. It was unlike him to be so distant. He explained that his absence was due in part to the fact that he had been going through a 'low period'. It all had been going so well, then he became frustrated with how long it had taken him to re-draft one of the chapters of his thesis. Disenchantment and disillusionment are part and parcel of the doctoral enterprise. For this student there was no point trying to talk about it: he just had to ride it out. 'The thing is if you went to the doctor and explained that you'd been experiencing highs of elation and euphoria [when the thesis was going well] and then bouts of resignation and depression you would probably be diagnosed as suffering from a mental health problem,' he said. Living with and through a PhD can certainly feel like some kind of bipolar affliction.

PhD supervision is one of academic life's year round staples, but what is supervision and when do you know it is being done well? These are things that are rarely talked about on campus. There are the obligatory 'professional development' courses that address the topic but I have rarely heard anyone comment on them being useful. Part of the problem is that

159

supervision is an allusive skill but equally our cognizance – as either supervisors or students – of what is actually happening in the room when supervision is taking place is at best partial.

I often find myself describing supervision as a kind of intellectual friendship that often extends far beyond the time it takes to write the thesis. This is not necessarily how it seems to doctoral students who recount a wide range of experiences. It is not uncommon for students to complain that being supervised is akin to a monthly intellectual interrogation that crushes rather than fosters confidence. For some time now I have been canvassing opinion, including that of my own supervisor Professor Pat Caplan. Pat was an extraordinary supervisor and discerning reader who helped many students along the doctoral road during the dark days of Thatcherism and through the austerity of the 1980s when I studied with her.

We hadn't seen each other for a while but meeting Pat always bears the antecedent trace of the many productive and fraught supervision sessions. This time I wanted to ask her about supervision itself. How would she describe it? 'You listen to them, you care about them . . . you give them time. You say the difficult things if you have to.'

In many respects I have simply tried to emulate these qualities as a supervisor. She facilitated the opening up of intellectual space in which my interests were admissible and legitimate. As supervisors I think there is an ethical responsibility to act as our best teachers and examples have acted. Pat was very supportive and encouraging but she was never afraid to say difficult things.

I remember visiting her for a supervision session at her north London home in the midst of a very bleak period of educational cuts during the mid-1980s. It was a time not unlike the atmosphere in higher education today. Clutching a draft paper I climbed the stairs and sat down in her study. There were very few jobs and the prospects for the future looked grim.

Thirty years later I can remember the conversation almost word for word.

'Les, I feel I must say this,' she said. 'I think you are talented and you have a lot to offer but I can't see a future for you and think you might be wasting your time continuing with the PhD.' I don't remember coming away from that meeting feeling demoralized. Rather, the lasting impression is how much courage it must have taken to say those things to a young person. She had the guts to say an uncomfortable truth as she saw it.

It wasn't a period when many people had much confidence in the future. I continued regardless and managed to complete my PhD largely due to the patient critical integrity of my supervisor. Pat's fears were not realized, partly through stubbornness and luck but mostly because of the improvement of the university's fortunes and an expansion of higher education over the last ten years that is now coming to a close. The point is that as supervisors we muster the best advice but we are not prophets.

As a student recently commented in a supervision meeting: 'I always assume that you have the answer in your head!' No, supervision is a place of deliberation and a time of thinking together, where potential answers are tossed around and tried out rather than transmitted from supervisor to student.

A student once complained, 'I can't write it in the way you want me to write it.' He missed the point. I was not trying to get him to write in a prescribed way but rather arrive at his own means of presenting his material and so enable his arguments to stand on their own terms. Repeated leaps of imagination are required in order to see how each piece might connect to the larger argument and the thesis as a whole; problems have to be formulated and reformulated and chapters are drafted and re-drafted over and over again. No wonder then that supervision – for student and supervisor alike – can seem exasperating, akin to wallpapering in a dark room!

What qualities make for a good supervisor? As I started to

ask students this question a range of things emerged, many of which surprised me. First, students said that a supervisor needs to be interested in and excited by the student's work. A sense of intellectual excitement conveys value to the student. Others said that, beyond this, it is important that the supervisor is still excited about scholarship and their vocation more broadly. Second, students want supervisors to listen attentively and read carefully and take time and not make the student feel like they are an inconvenience to be dispensed with as quickly as possible. Good supervisors need to be patient and not teach everything they know but rather encourage students to arrive at answers for themselves. Part of the value of supervision is that the doctoral student has to give an account of him/herself and their project on a regular basis. Sometimes this involves convincing themselves, as much as their supervisors, that they are progressing and moving closer to the completion of the project. Third, good supervisors are honest in their criticism but constructive. In this sense, the supervisor needs to be both partisan and supportive of the project but, at the same time, its most loyal and trenchant critic. The supervisor is the student's first and most committed reader. A student who submitted her thesis recently put it this way: 'Sometimes I find it funny how I always say "I have to write a chapter for Les" rather than "I have to write a chapter for my PhD" . . . You start to internalize your supervisor's voice. If a chapter isn't working and I think "What would Les say?" then that helps me to fix it.' Fourth, supervisors should enable students to explore ideas but not let them drift too much. In this sense supervisors need to remind the student of the stages of the thesis as a whole and the larger time frame. Finally, the best supervisors are ones who also keep the longer-term future of the student in mind in terms of academic and intellectual development, but also of what might come next in terms of a working life after the PhD.

What qualities by comparison make for a good PhD student? A cynical or self-serving faculty member might say a good PhD student is someone who leaves the supervisor alone and produces an immaculately conceived PhD after three years of lonely industry. A PhD student needs to read widely and imaginatively and this is perhaps the first quality a good student needs to cultivate. Second, a student needs 'mobility' and they need to engage with the world. As one colleague put it, they should 'step out into the streets with their books with them'. Mark C. Taylor puts it to his students in these terms: 'Do not do what I do; rather, take whatever I have to offer and do with it what I could never imagine doing and then come back and tell me about it.' Third, PhD students need to write regularly and to write to deadlines. This is a much harder skill to cultivate than it might appear at first sight because writing can often be a real struggle. The progress of a project is not measured in the ability of a student to 'talk their thesis', rather it is calculated in words amassed, chapters drafted and how much of the whole thesis has been committed to the hard drive and then to paper. Fourth, the hallmark of a good student is the capacity to hear criticism and react to it productively. Supervisors sometimes repeat the same critical points over and over and wait, sometimes in vain, for the student to act on them. Assimilating critical feedback and acting on it is an important skill that is not at all straightforward. Finally, in order to complete the PhD students need to remain loyal to their project. It is a long process and the temptation to become distracted by a short-term gain and interesting side projects can be very strong. In this sense, students need to remain vigilant about making the completion of the PhD their first intellectual priority. The thesis itself is often much more than a three-year project; it's the beginning of a much larger intellectual venture that will evolve and change over a lifetime of scholarship.

The committed and critical form of intellectual dialogue that takes place in PhD supervision is among the most rewarding aspects of the intellectual vocation but it can also be mysterious, fragile and risky. Student and supervisor, each in different ways, put their ideas and judgements to the test and open themselves up to critical scrutiny. When the student eventually goes before her examiners in the viva voce she isn't alone: the advice and judgements of her supervisor are also being assessed with her. This is acknowledged by the examiners because they read the thesis not only for the candidate's ideas but also to see if the student has been well advised about form and structure. Examiners might explain or even condone the weaknesses of a thesis because 'it wasn't supervised properly' or the student 'should never been allowed to submit'. As a supervisor you can never really be sure that you are getting it right. Also, the reactions or behaviour of students don't always feel like appreciation. I know that some of the actions of my own supervisor that I hold up as an example to emulate are not quite how she reflects upon them.

A few years ago I wrote an article for a newspaper that included a discussion of how difficult and painful it was to read my supervisor's critical comments on the literary shortcomings of early drafts of my thesis. The piece included what I thought were some quite nice metaphors – 'red pen marks like a form of intellectual bloodletting', for example. I sent the piece to Pat expecting the comments to raise a wry smile. When the article arrived through her letterbox she was nearing the end of her career as a supervisor and reflecting on her life as a university teacher. She feared that the article might be evidence of a longstanding grudge and I am ashamed to say I think it hurt her.

I mention this as an example of the vulnerabilities at play in the supervisory relationship that are by no means confined to the student. Along the way both students and supervisors will make mistakes. By the same token, they will get many things right. Together they will get to the end of the thesis which in many respects is not an end in itself but a beginning. It is the beginning of a scholarly career but it is also a moment to formulate, assess and reproduce the ethics of scholarship itself. The former student will carry what they have learned by example. They might also decide to do things differently as through the course of time they in turn become supervisors.

Thinking Together

Recently, I spent the morning at a local south London further education college. The college provides a place of refuge and hope for what used to be called 'non-traditional students'. It is not an easy educational environment to work in and opportunity and alternative futures are forged here often amid social damage and self-destruction. It's an extraordinary place in which many lives are changed while other young people are broken and trapped within cycles of violence where the perpetrators are culturally and socially the mirror image of their victims. I come for an open discussion with students who are preparing to go onto higher education; I do this every year.

The rules of dialogue are always the same although the items on the agenda vary. The students, who are on a youth access to higher education programme, prepare a set of questions beforehand. The questions range from big ones about world politics to the sociological minutiae of a specific theory on the syllabus. Each student takes responsibility for asking one question. I get handed the list of questions just before we start.

We talk sometimes for two hours without a break. The sessions are always extraordinary: I learn something from them

166

and I hope that they in turn learn something too. They always ask the biggest, most important and direct questions. They suffer no fools and if you are not interesting or genuine, then the loss of their attention is felt almost physically like someone letting go of your hand.

A young black person inquires. 'You're obviously a white man . . . but you write a lot about race. Was it through sociology that you developed an affinity with people of colour?' I can see his candour makes his teacher uneasy. I try to be as honest as I can. I tell him it wasn't just through education but through friendships in my youth with black people, largely the result of playing sport, that I shaped my own interests and commitments. It was also hearing racism in my own family. He seems to recognize the streets and places I talk about and maybe some of the kinds of people I describe. I say that sociology has provided a way to make sense of some of the things that I experienced as a young person that I couldn't understand. Pausing, I say, 'I don't know if that makes any sense.' He nods and takes his clenched fists and taps his chest just above his heart.

We talk about what young people fear and love about south London's 'grime' and 'endz'. I tell them that things seem so different now to me as a middle-aged person interested in what's happening to young people. 'Tell me if I am wrong but it seems to me that for some young people the world is shrinking and getting smaller – scared to take a bus ride because it takes them into the wrong postcode.' Excited and intense argument ensues. A young woman says, 'Yeah, I think you are right and the thing is it is we . . . we who is doing it to we.' The students think aloud, expressing what's on their minds within a group that recognizes the relevance of today's syllabus all too well.

Next question: 'Can sociology change society?' No, society isn't changed by sociology or thinking but perhaps we are changing ourselves. I try to offer them some examples where social research has influenced society positively but also examples where sociology has acted as racism's accomplice. We are changed by 'living in books' and by entering into such conversations and thinking together but also by opening out to the social world and having our understandings challenged as a result. This is not the arrogant certainty that has the last word; nor the capacity to translate or transpose the world through sociological revelation or that which privileges sociological thought as the key to unlock common sense. It is close to what philosopher Romand Coles calls a dialogical ethics, or the give and take of a receptive generosity that both hears and speaks. Every year it's alive in that room.

The Doublethink of Open Access

Writers rightly have a special love of words. They matter to us because they provide our refuge and perhaps the only place where we feel truly at home. As George Orwell pointed out, damaging their meaning violates thought and by extension often re-orders relations between people. In *Nineteen Eighty-Four* Orwell calls the process of making words come to mean their exact opposite 'doublethink'. In his dystopian image of Britain's future The Ministry of Love spews hateful propaganda, The Ministry of Truth produces dishonesties and The Ministry of Peace concerns itself with perpetual war.

Doublethink is alive in today's university environment. The pervasive language of 'transparency' is really producing more secrecy, where we are frightened to write anything in an email that we wouldn't be prepared to put on a notice board. Arguments made by an appeal for more 'openness' often result in more enclosures and boundaries. So it is with 'Open Access' publishing.

On the surface how could any writer quarrel with the idea that their work should be more available and accessible? After all, don't we all write to be read? If academics are funded publically to produce knowledge shouldn't it be available to the public? Pay-walled academic journals can charge as much as £20–30 for a single article. Sociologist John Holmwood comments that while the 'case for open access appears overwhelming' it has in fact a misleading appeal.

Holmwood explains that the driver to make knowledge 'open access' is not the public good but rather commercial interest. The shift towards open access is happening at the precise moment when educational policy is stressing the interests of business and making academic knowledge available to commercial exploitation. Open access licences effectively enable entrepreneurs to access for free research-based forms of knowledge that are often subsidized by public investment.

Indeed, in this model the cost for making knowledge open access will be met by the universities, and ultimately the academic researchers because the journals they publish in require payment for opening up the content. This also means that pressure will be placed on universities to foot the bill and choices will need to be made about which publications and authors will be included in this version of 'openness'. So, paradoxically, the move to open access will make some academic work widely available, while less profitable forms of knowledge remain enclosed behind expensive journal pay-walls.

There is another dimension to the debate about open access that threatens the university as a whole. Many academics – including myself – have been enthusiastic about the possibilities offered by making lectures and podcasts available for free online. The idea that students can download and listen again to their lectures on their iPods or mobile phones has potential to let ideas travel and be heard in new ways. Again this seems like an unqualified positive opportunity.

The problem lies in what this means in a context where stark divisions are emerging between institutions across the higher education sector. The experience of the charismatic Princeton sociologist Mitch Duneier offers a cautionary tale.

In the summer of 2012 he offered his introductory course in sociology for free through the online provider Coursera. The results were staggering and the course attracted 40,000 students from 113 countries. Duneier became a MOOC (Massive Open Online Courses) star.

The course enabled the communication of sociological ideas to new audiences as well as dialogue with the students who accessed the course remotely. Duneier reflected: 'Within three weeks I had received more feedback on my sociological ideas than I had in a career of teaching.' Mitch's course seemed like a perfect example of the positive potential of openness. However, when Coursera opened its content for free use within the University System of Maryland and other state universities, it became clear that they were being used to cut costs. Free online content was 'blended' with a reduced amount of face-to-face contact with sociologists available locally. MOOCs had enabled cuts in public education, while offering the justification that students had open access to world-class academics in Ivy League schools.

As result, Mitch Duneier withdrew his sociology MOOC, reporting that he had been unwittingly used to cut costs and undermine his sociological colleagues in public universities. He told *The Chronicle of Higher Education*: 'I . . . don't want to be part of a movement that is really about helping state universities achieve cost savings at the expense of their own faculty and students.'

What emerges is the need and necessity to consider not just the meanings of openness but the context within which writing and creative work occurs within the university. This involves a critical assessment of both scholarly work and how its value is measured and judged but also the condition under which academic writers labour. Given the longstanding attention of feminist scholars and writers to the relationship between the personal and political dimensions of intellectual work it shouldn't be surprising that they have been at the forefront of the discussion of scholarly praxis.

My Goldsmiths colleague Sarah Kember argues that there is a need to 'open out from open access'. Such a move would pre-empt the re-enclosure of knowledge or its assimilation back into the logic of measuring academic value within the audit culture. Here the traditions of feminist deconstruction offer tools to unpick the doublethink of open access. Kember issues a stirring invitation to 'unwork the work of writing about scholarly practice and to work harder at the work of writing out of its enclosures'.

This also invites the ultimate question of what is at stake in our scholarly work. Why write, Kember asks provocatively? Her answer is that we should write to transform the space of writing itself and the conditions, conventions and confinements – including forms of self-regulation – that operate within it. This is not just an argument for experimental forms of work but rather for fostering a feminist ethos of experimenting in scholarship. As a leading force in the setting up of Goldsmiths Press, Sarah Kember has done precisely this, creating new publishing opportunities and spaces for writing.

The happy consequence for me is that the press is providing a published home for orphaned ideas like this diary.

Against Intellectual Suicide

Today I did an interview with a young academic who is editing a book of portraits of contemporary sociologists. I took her request to be featured among them as a compliment and I guess it comes from reaching a particular age and a certain stage in an academic life. The interview was an enjoyable experience and an opportunity to try and make sense of my own eccentric journey through academic life.

At one point my interviewer asked if I had any advice to offer younger academics. On occasions like this I often struggle to find any words of helpful guidance. This is not just the result of an in-growing sense of humility. It is also the nagging fact that I know I have played the academic game badly in some respects. I know my score on some of the key measures of academic status – like the H Index metric that correlates the number of citations of our work against the number of journal articles we publish – is much lower than it should be. This is a result of not harvesting large numbers of article citations in the right journals. So I know – in these terms – my example is not one to follow.

Part of the point of academic metrics is to make us as employees feel like we are failing even when we are killing ourselves to succeed. The corporatizing impulse is transforming the university and it is hard not to become possessed by these measures of intellectual value and worth. What struck me as I thought about what to say in answer to my young colleague is the importance of trying to defend the value of reading and thinking together against these limited ways of defining what is good. It means defending each other too and it is not an overstatement to say that the challenge we face is how to avoid committing either institutional or intellectual suicide.

There is a way to navigate a course that is something like this: be mindful of those formats, spaces and kinds of research writing that are valued within the hierarchies of the audit culture. It is unspoken but it is an open secret. There is a hierarchy of value and the hierarchy changes around a bit but we know that somewhere at the top of that hierarchy of value is publishing in the key disciplinary journals of whatever field you are in. Then comes writing monographic books – we know that is high up in the hierarchy of value too – and then things that are in the lower gradations are book chapters, online journalism and probably last of all blog posts.

Does that mean you only do those things that are valued within the hierarchy I have just described? I think that is a heart-breaking recipe for intellectual mortification. On the one hand, it is important to do things that are going to help young researchers make that transition into their first academic jobs. At the same time they have to keep their intellectual passions alive and curiosities awake. I have tried to keep both impulses alive but I have probably made the mistake of putting too much energy into formats that simply do not count and cannot be accounted for with the structures of academic audit.

I remember turning up to give a keynote lecture some years ago. The person charged with introducing me had done his homework for the introduction. He turned to me as said with surprise: 'Oh you've got a lot of online publications?' The implication was: are you sure you should be wasting your time on such things? I don't think paper formats will dominate the structures of auditing value in the academy for much longer. I just don't think that they can. Something will have to give because there is so much sociological life in digital spaces of what we refer to as alternative media.

If all you care about is your next article in *Theory, Culture and Society* (TCS) – and incidentally I do care about those things too – then you have foreclosed that possibility. I think younger scholars are much more in touch with those possibilities and watching them do great things makes me incredibly hopeful. Even the most prestigious journals like TCS know they have opportunities to be more inventive now and you can see that on their new website.

There is a wonderful project that Mark Carrigan does called *The Sociological Imagination* (http://sociologicalimagination.org), which is a website and Twitter feed, and you get news from *Sociological Imagination* every day. He is a postgraduate student who will have graduated by the time this book is published. He is just somebody who is passionate and curious about sociology. He is interested in interesting things and he has got thousands of people following him and following what he is doing, and old lags like me saying, 'You know, I would like to join in too.'

The energy that is in these online spaces of academic writing is not timid and it is not conservative. The level of public engagement and number of people following their passions and communicating things that they are interested in is inspiring. There is something about that which I find incredibly nourishing and important. But I would also say to those young colleagues – remember what counts and who is doing the counting.

The Summer

Silence Please – Exam in Progress

I think the devil must be in command of the weather during the exam season. The hottest, most uncomfortably humid conditions arrive just in time for the biggest exam days. The high pressure combined with student stress can make for a particularly fraught and difficult week on campus.

I know some people think invigilation is a tremendous waste of resources and that members of staff should use their time more productively. Perhaps our time could be better served but invigilation also has its own reward. Wandering up and down the aisle, invigilators do next to nothing other than hand out additional sheets of paper and pieces of string necessary to tie the extra pages to the exam script.

As the students rack their brains, a cloud of serious thinking hangs over them and the calm of the exam room gives the invigilator space for their own thoughts too. Let's face it, the licence to do nothing is a rare luxury amid the frantic hubbub of academic life. Invigilation insists on a kind of institutional idleness. Well, most of the time.

The quiet can be difficult to maintain particularly on an urban campus like Goldsmiths, in the middle of noisy New Cross, south London. It is a blistering hot afternoon in early

Silence Please – Exam in Progress

June and I've been called to act as a standby invigilator for the media studies department. Candidates get down to the job of thinking and scribbling as I look forward to a couple of hours of purposeless contemplation. A larger significance is contained in the fragile stillness of the exam room.

Sociologist Fran Tonkiss wrote: 'The Babel of the crowd and the wordless solitude of the individual in a noisy city capture in sound a larger urban tension between collective and subjective life. Sometimes it can be . . . hard even to listen to one's own thoughts, amongst all the noise.' We need to block out the throng of collective activity to hear ourselves think.

Today the background noise of the city seems at a much higher pitch than usual. I start to make an aural inventory: the sound of the jets passing overhead, the incessant police sirens, a helicopter buzzing probably monitoring the traffic, a distant door slamming, a group of excited students whose laughter is suddenly muted after a member of staff says reproachfully, 'Shsssh, there is an exam in progress!'

Then an additional intrusion seeps into the exam room's soundscape. This is a sound too far! A high operatic voice repeats a melody over and over, each time more out of tune than the last. It is excruciating, a vocal equivalent of sharp fingernails being dragged slowly over a blackboard. The pained look on one young woman's face says it all. She puts up her hand and I walk over. I whisper, 'Do you want me to try and do something about that racket?' She nods pathetically like someone suffering from a mild dose of the flu.

I head off to find the tuneless singer but this, it turns out, is easier said than done. The voice seems to be everywhere and nowhere. I follow my ears. The singer is in full blast at an appallingly high and ill-pitched frequency. Every time I feel like I am getting close it goes quieter again. As I turn another corner it seems to get louder. There is no pattern, like some tortuous parlour game of sonic hide-and-seek.

I try the floor above but still the voice remains evasive. I head in desperation for the music department some distance from where the exam is actually taking place. Where could the voice possibly be coming from? The secretary points me in the direction of a rehearsal room two floors below where the exam is being held. As I follow the directions the piercing voice gets louder; this time I am on the right track. There are about a dozen practice rooms all in a line. The tuneless offender's discordant tones are emanating from Room 12. I knock. A small blonde-haired music student opens the door. It seems impossible that such an incredible din can be coming from such a slight frame. I tell her that there is an exam going on upstairs. 'Ooh sorry,' she says. 'I'll come back later.'

It's probably taken twenty minutes to track down the culprit but it feels more like an hour. The exertion of running up and down stairs in the heat means I am 'glowing' slightly. The student who made the initial complaint still has a pained expression on her face, the anguish probably induced by an ambiguously worded question on the paper. At least it is quiet now – well, except for the jet engines, police sirens and the new addition of a barking dog!

And then . . . Oh no, not again: another uninvited guest in the sonic shape of a jazz saxophone. The melody is perfect but a chorus of sighs from the long-suffering students meets this rendition of Charlie Parker's 'Cool Blues'. I know where the guilty party is hiding and a few minutes later calm is restored. Returning to the exam room I pick up some pieces of string and sheets of extra paper and resume invigilation responsibilities, luxuriating in the relative peace of idle contemplation.

The Exam Board

The annual exam board is perhaps the most bizarre spectacle in the academic calendar. Each department has a board dedicated to its own discipline composed of all the markers – these are the ones in the room with bags under their bleary eyes – who have scrutinized the student work that is listed in fat piles of listed marks and tables. Thirty staff sit around a table like intelligent mannequins listening – or simulating attention – to the student numbers and grades being read out while they follow silently the lists of candidates' results.

It can sometimes seem endless, made worse by the board's secret languages of abbreviations and codes: 'The student has two and a half units at level two and the failure of SOZ0245 is condoned so that can proceed as a Z1.' Only the exams officer and the chair fully understand what the hell it all means.

Then there are the perennial grumbles of external examiners whose volume of work increases year on year while the turnaround time for reading the volumes of scripts shrinks. There is always an inscrutable college administrator, a veteran of innumerable exam boards, who has an eye for an overlooked technicality or who can be called upon to predict the judgement of the university's higher authorities.

They are usually tranquil occasions in contrast to the frantic rush to get the marks in and assemble the packages of assessments to send to the external examiners. But exam boards can have moments of drama.

A friend told me of one board where the exams officer – a 'high profile' academic who considered 'administration' a waste of his intellect – had not done the significant amount of work required to prepare for the board. Chaos and uproar ensued, the external examiner resigned on the spot and tempers flared producing a kind of academic civic unrest. This is exceptionally rare.

Usually, though, it is students who are on the boundaries between degree classifications that raise the emotional temperature of the board, especially when a student is denied a first class degree by the tiniest of margins. Despite the public concern about 'grade inflation' and falling university standards, the best students have long been denied the grades they deserve. I remember once sitting on a board as an external examiner when an academic – who was retiring – said of a student dissertation that it was 'the best piece of work [he'd] read' in his more than forty years as a university teacher. He gave the dissertation 72. That is 28 points off the possible maximum!

Historically even the best teachers have not used the top quarter of the marking spectrum. Examiners' inhibitions and the hugging of grade borders create marginal cases where the best students suffer. By the time of the exam board, with its strict rules, it is too late and there is often little room for manoeuvre. You can't put right in June or July at the board that which could have been easily rectified with a flick of the marker's pencil.

To my mind markers should use the full range and avoid hedging their bets. Perhaps, there is something here about boundary maintenance in the reluctance to award high marks.

The Exam Board

A 72 keeps the brightest students in their place – as pupils not peers.

In 2009 figures were released showing that between the years 1996/97 and 2007/08 the proportion of first class degrees awarded had almost doubled, with 13.3% of all graduates receiving a First. Despite the protests of grade devaluation this is a sign of progress. I am sure that despite the trend there were many hidden cases where the inhibitions of markers meant that degree finalists missed the highest achievement by the smallest of margins.

On the Occasion of Retirement

For academics retirement is fast becoming a thing of the past. The normal pension age is 65 under the UK's University Superannuation Scheme (USS). However, from 2011 'flexible' forms of retirement have been introduced making it possible for academics to work on almost indefinitely. It conjures an image of piles of unmarked exam scripts on top of a lapsed faculty member's coffin, accompanied by an irritated email enquiry as to 'why the grades for this course haven't been returned before the deadline!' Flexible retirement will mean our in-boxes follow us into the grave.

Since retiring from the University of Leeds in 1990 Zygmunt Bauman has entered into the most prolific period of his life. Publishing one acclaimed book after another, he is one of the most important thinkers of our time and has attracted non-academic readers too. In 2012 Bauman wrote 'my curiosity refuses to retire'. A paradox in academic life is that we often have to get away from our jobs to actually do our work. So, retirement can mean being relieved of professional duties and the freedom to think and reflect. Zygmunt Bauman has published thirty books in his 'retirement'. His example was very much on my mind in preparing to say a few words in

185

the summer of 2011 at a gathering to mark the retirement of Professor Vic Seidler from teaching at Goldsmiths.

Vic was offered a job at Goldsmiths in 1971. He had just returned from Boston when he received a call from Sue Steadman-Jones offering him a part-time job teaching social philosophy. There was only one condition: he had to start the very next day. I think this title – social philosopher – is a pretty apt way to characterize Vic's thought. Social involvement equally combined with philosophical engagement.

A part-time position was attractive because it enabled Vic to combine academic work and teaching with his varied political involvements in workers' movements, student politics and anti-sexism. I think that this combination is something that really characterizes Vic's way of being an intellectual. It wasn't until 1976 that he took up a full-time position at the College because, as he told me recently, 'you wouldn't be taken seriously if you didn't have a full-time job'.

This meant that from the very beginning of his academic career Vic did not see himself as confined to British sociology; rather, his sociological imagination was always more international and philosophically adventurous. Also, I think it meant that he saw teaching as his key commitment, his first principle.

I first met Vic in 1982. He used to teach a second year course on social theory. It took place in an old tiered lecture theatre. I remember the seating was almost like being confronted with a wall of benches, staggered at about 60 degrees. Anyhow, my friend Sim Colton and I, neither of us sociology students, would arrive early and smuggle ourselves in at the back of the lecture theatre, hoping not to be noticed.

In those days it was a twelve-week course: the first half focused on Karl Marx's writings; and the second was dedicated to Sigmund Freud's thought. Vic would come in and make some announcements. Then he would start to talk using no notes. He would explain the intricacies of Marx's theory of alienation or Freud's conceptualization of the unconscious, one lucid sentence after another. All the while he would pace up and down in front of us, as if he was taking these ideas for a walk. Sim and I used to say to each other afterwards: 'How does he do that!' Watching him teach or give a paper now, I am still struck by that same sense of wonder.

Although neither Sim nor I were officially his students, we'd go for meetings and tutorials with him. Sim grew up in Manchester and his father worked in the printing industry. His mother died when he was very young. After the bereavement his father had to fight to keep Sim and his four brothers together: social workers wanted to put them in care, claiming that their father wouldn't be able to cope.

The boys developed a deep sense of solidarity and fierce suspicion of powerful institutions. His home was like an extension of the print shop floor – I won't repeat the kind of industrial language that was exchanged over whose turn it was to do the washing or to make the tea.

Sim would go and see Vic to try and figure out how to understand his own life, or how to frame it – this is one of Vic's favourite phrases – within the complex interplay between masculinity, generation and class. I saw Sim recently at his father's funeral. His Dad had lived an extraordinary life and in retirement he had painted, written poetry and would offer a recital of Rudyard Kipling's 'If' at a drop of hat (drunk or sober).

Sim recalled those tutorials with Vic in the heyday of Thatcherism. He described going into his office in the front of 47 Lewisham Way. You would go in, books and papers would be everywhere, a Persian rug on the floor, a picture of Freud on one wall and Marx on the other. Vic would be in a chair at the centre of all the piles of papers and books, often wearing on his feet a pair of slippers.

Vic is interested in you but also in what you are interested in. This interest always conveyed such a sense of being valued.

On the Occasion of Retirement

Simone Weil, one of Vic's early influences, wrote: '"You don't interest me." No man can say these words to another without committing a cruelty and offending against justice.' I think these words have guided Vic's way of practising a sociological vocation.

The other thing that he taught us very early on is that there is no hope of changing the world or even understanding it better, without first trying to change ourselves. Sim actually appeared as a 'case study' in a book by Harry Christian – one of Vic's associates – called *The Making of Anti-Sexist Men*.

Vic's political commitments made him a writer. He writes not because his academic position expects it but because he has something to say and communicate. He has published on an astonishing range of topics including social theory, emotions, masculinity, fatherhood, philosophy, sexual politics, anti-Semitism, the Shoah, terrorism, multiculturalism, faith, ecology, youth, Latin American culture, narrative and memory, history and mourning. He writes because he is trying to work something out.

It is an indication of the lasting relevance of his work that Routledge has republished six of his books within their 'Routledge Revival' series. For once they got something right. There is a shift in Vic's writing from the universalism of his poster boys – Marx and Freud – and a dogmatic version of Left politics, to an engagement with difference. A characteristic of his recent work is openness and a measure of humility in what we can claim to know, while at the same time a commitment to social critique.

Finally, being around him, at a conference or in an intellectual conversation, Vic always conveys a sense of intellectual excitement, a kind of enchantment in and with ideas. You can always rely on him to support an event and to ask a question. Sometimes we almost have to restrain his enthusiasm and excitement.

Aeschylus wrote that to 'learn is to be young, however old'. For Vic, this has always been learning with students, through what they are interested in and what they bring with them into the seminar room. One thing for sure is that it has kept him young and maybe this is why he does not seem to have aged in the thirty years I have known him.

Vic is interested in new ideas but not in the performance of intelligence, or what he referred to recently as 'the self-important talking to the self-important'. There are some aspects of the new academic environment that he's less at home in. He never quite took to email, for example. There is a kind of gentle stubbornness in Vic.

On the other hand, it makes total sense to me that he is an avid user of SMS and text messaging – an authored person-to-person communication both intimate and social. That's why Vic has his mobile phone always to hand.

Writers like Vic Seidler and Zygmunt Bauman have escaped the trappings of 'flexible retirement' in order to do their work more vigorously. It is perhaps ironic that giving up their professional responsibilities has made them more focused and committed to their craft. Of the many things I have learned from Vic, three in particular stand out: 1) convey to students a sense of profound interest in them and their interests; 2) write about things that matter to you; 3) retain a sense of enchantment and excitement in ideas. I have learned many other things from him but I think these three are the most precious.

The Writer's Desk

In the summer of 2005 Italian sculptor Giancarlo Neri installed his huge 30-foot sculpture 'The Writer' on Parliament Hill, part of Hampstead Heath in north London. Neri's tribute to the lonely heroism of writing took the form of a monumental vacant wooden table and chair. The giant sculpture, made of six tons of steel and 1,000 pounds of wood, was an uncanny presence set against the sunburnt grass and trees of London's historic park where Karl Marx liked to walk on Sundays. It was an apt location for the work, given the many literary Gullivers who lived and wrote in this part of north London, including Keats, Coleridge, Freud and C.L.R. James.

'As one moves around the elongated table legs and looks up from under the table' wrote critics Nirmal Puwar and Sanjay Sharma, 'the weight of the world as it is carried by the labour of writers, overwhelms, tires and leaves one wondering.' The striking sculpture, so out of place, brings to the foreground the 'where' of writing.

For many great writers like Marx it had to be one specific place, in his case desk 07 in the British Library's Reading Room. Freud, a refugee from Nazi Germany, would recreate his writing desk wherever he ended up. His cluttered desk at the Freud Museum in nearby Hampstead is packed with ancient sculptures in wood and bronze of idols, gods and deities from Egypt, China, Greece and Rome which looked back at him from the edges of the table. He saw collecting them as one of his main addictions alongside his famous penchant for smoking cigars. He needed to surround himself with carved friends and ghoulish idols in order to put pen to paper.

Georges Perec wrote that he liked his desk to be 'cluttered, almost to excess'. Tidying up marked for him the beginning and the end of a writing project. 'At such times I dream of an immaculate, unsullied desktop, with everything in the right place and nothing unnecessary on it,' he wrote. 'Nothing protruding from it, with all my pencils sharpened (but why do I have more than one pencil? I can see six of them, at a glance!), with all my papers in piles, or even better, with no papers on it at all, just a notebook open at a fresh page.' Like him, I think and write surrounded by mess punctuated by brief binges of tidiness. Brief periods of order mark the end of one thing and the beginning of something else.

I often need my books around me in order to write, the names on their spines peering back like Freud's sculptures. I don't order the books on the shelves: somehow the anarchic contiguity – Harper Lee rubbing covers with Clifford Geertz – is intellectually productive and pleasing. I simply can't work in the same place all the time and recently I have developed an allergic reaction to my desk.

I think part of this aversion is linked to the restlessness and frustration inherent in the act of writing. The time spent reading and priming one's mind is always as long, if not longer, than the period spent hammering out the words on the keyboard. Walking away from the desk or finding a new place to write is part of that process of writing preparation. This is not an individual problem or foible.

Marxist historian Eric Hobsbawm had a house close to

The Writer's Desk

Hampstead Heath in which he used three studies and seven writing desks, including a white children's one that he bought for his daughter to do her homework on. Jill Krementz's wonderful book of photographs *The Writer's Desk* captures the workplaces of an inspiring range of authors, from Eudora Welty to Ralph Ellison.

John Updike's introduction comments that he looks at these photographs with 'a prurient interest, the way that I might look at the beds of notorious courtesans'. Updike confesses to having three desks, each supporting a different activity: an oak desk where he answers letters and talks on the telephone; an olive, drab, steel military desk where he does delicate writing (poems or the beginning of a novel) by hand with a pencil; and lastly, a white Formica-veneered table dedicated to the practical industry of word processing and typing up. 'Being able to move from desk to desk, like being able to turn over in bed, solves some cramps and fidgets and stratifies the authorial persona,' Updike concludes.

Many authors like Katherine Anne Porter need a cup of strong black coffee to start the day, but what is striking about Krementz's book is the incredible diversity in the writers' preferred surroundings. Jean Piaget and Dorothy West need mess and organized chaos while Edmund White and E.B. White compose their sentences in rooms that are virtually paper free. Saul Bellow and Rita Dove put pen to paper on their feet at standing desks while Walker Percy and Cathleen Schine write their books in bed. For other writers it's a matter of physically getting away from all that is familiar and finding a writing desk in a remote village or a grand metropolis in which they can be anonymous. We each need to find our own way of furnishing a productive literary environment.

The other thing that is striking about Neri's magnificent desk monument is the way it suggests the proliferation of places where authors can write. In the age of the laptop computer writers are no longer hostage to the immobile typewriter and a desk can be found almost anywhere as long as the battery is charged or if there is a compatible mains socket close at hand. This points to another dimension of the desk allergy syndrome that stems from the nature of life in the twenty-first century.

The alchemy of wi-fi hot spots and the global reach of email make it almost impossible to escape academic responsibilities for longer than the duration of a plane flight and that too will soon be a thing of the past. Connectivity offers a staggering capacity for writers to access information. The price we pay for this resource that has so quickly been taken for granted is the exasperation of seemingly endless queries about meetings, essays and deadlines. The academic life has become open access. In order to think and write I find myself seeking out places to disconnect and get off the information superhighway.

Today I am in my current favourite spot, Pistachios in the Park Café on Hilly Fields, one of south London's most beautiful – and lesser known – parks. I find it an ideal location to get my laptop out and write. It is located almost exactly halfway between where I live and where I work. It literalizes aptly the place of writing in my own life: a vocation that is between what I get paid to do and the rest of my life.

Now I am surrounded by the sounds of toddlers crying, young Mums laughing over the absurdities of parenting and dogs barking loudly. 'Don't you find it distracting?' asks Fred, the owner. Truth is I don't. On odd occasions explosions of mirth from sixth-formers gathered around laptops watching comic YouTube virals disrupt my concentration, but those are exceptional lapses. The visitors to the café are busy getting on with more important things and are not asking for an immediate reply to email inquiry.

Freud's desk seems less strange now as I settle down to work. The people here are not mute carved figures. They are busy getting on with their own lives and are not asking for an immediate reply to email inquiry. The person tapping away at a laptop in these public places nonetheless draws comfort and inspiration from them. It helps counteract inhibitions of authorial self-consciousness, which can be so stifling. It gets me started and helps me keep moving with the work. The noise of the children playing is also a reminder that writing is a profoundly social activity; it connects my thoughts to yours. In short, it lets them travel.

The Library Angel

I have always thought that a library is a place of refuge. The quiet reflection afforded there has a special role both in creating a space of learning but also in living differently. For the poor who lack the room to think, a public library often sits between their cramped domestic arrangements and the noisy free flow of the street. Richard Hoggart wrote that the public library, as a consequence, becomes a 'home from home', somewhere not just to compose your thoughts but also to remake yourself.

In the thirties Hoggart, a working-class grammar school boy from Yorkshire, frequented Hunslet Public Library where he read books in a warm room and borrowed them without charge. He wrote in his memoir that 'a great many people from poor backgrounds have paid tribute to the place of the public libraries in their unofficial education'. A library is precious to them because they lived in homes without books.

In 2010 The Rolling Stones' Keith Richards told an audience at the New York Public Library that libraries were the only places where he 'willingly obeyed the rules'. For the guitarist, who had a fraught relationship with school, post-war Dartford was a bleak and inhospitable place to come of age but the Victorian splendour of the public library was the exception. Many libraries were built after the passing of the Public Libraries Act in 1850, when, in response to political pressure begun by the Chartists, public libraries aimed to give workers gainful recreation. The reforms also aimed to dissipate revolutionary dissent by providing public education in every town. Keith Richards told the New Yorkers: 'It was a sort of different space . . . it was there for everybody. I could find out things I wasn't being taught in school. It was like the centre of things and so it should be.'

A library is a place of refuge. It shouldn't be surprising that asylum seekers and refugees use libraries to cope with the limitations placed on them like the prohibition against them working. Forced to live in a state of mortifying idleness and endless waiting they often visit the library. Katherine Robinson documents encounters with asylum seekers in her research on Brigstock Road Library, Croydon. Here migrants animate their days browsing the stacks of books, surfing the internet and reading newspapers. Toni Morrison says that public libraries stand alone not only in offering free access to knowledge but also as an open space for life in public. In libraries, she writes, 'No tuition is charged, no oath sworn, no visa demanded.' This openness conveys to all in society a message that, in her words, says: 'touch me, use me, my hush is not indifference, my space is not a barrier'.

A grand citadel made of books like the New York Public Library is a symbol of power too. In *Go Tell It On the Mountain* James Baldwin's central character John Grimes does not dare to enter it because he sees it as a bastion of whiteness. Grimes holds a library card but fears to go inside because 'all the white people would look at him with pity'. He turns away from the entrance and decides instead to return to his neighbourhood library. He consoles himself with the thought that once he has read 'all the books uptown' he will have the 'poise' to go into the library in downtown Manhattan. Baldwin's book, published in 1953, speaks brilliantly to the internalized doubts produced by growing up in a racially segregated and class divided world. Today the New York Public Library houses a collection of Baldwin's letters, personal papers and manuscripts. John Grimes made it inside finally.

A local public library then is a stepping stone, a place to reckon with educational vertigo and gain confidence. As a boy in the 1970s I spent so many hours in the New Addington Public Library that the librarian – a kindly but stern woman – would bring me a cup of tea when she made one for herself. She took pity on the boy in the corner and bent the rules – food and drink were strictly prohibited in those days. There was zero tolerance of noise too above the rustle of newspaper pages being turned.

The architecture of that library had none of the great Victorian grandeur described by Hoggart and Richards but projected lower aspirations. It was opened on 22 June 1964 as part of a new community complex that also included a swimming baths. The public library was a municipal token of educational opportunity linked to the new comprehensive schools where the children from the estate were educated. The roof was jagged like the teeth of a saw and its large glass panels gave the library a light and airy feel. Architecturally it was the civic equivalent of the post-war council houses in which the estates' residents lived – functional, clean but modest.

During the day old-age pensioners would negotiate the difficult task of steering their shopping trolleys through the library's revolving door. Many came in search of large-print books. The way to cope with a reader's failing eyesight was simply to enlarge the print. The upgrading of Catherine Cookson's *The Cinder Path* or Daphne du Maurier's *Jamaica Inn* to multi-volume literary epics seemed somehow faintly comic.

A children's section was to the left of the issue desk, catering for the opposite end of the estate's demographic. This area had lower stacks for the children's books, nursery chairs and tables and a box of toys. Occasionally the silence of the library would be punctured by the children's innocent mirth. The calm would be quickly repaired, usually with a parent saying, 'Shush, you can't do that – we're in the library now.'

The building had a permanent smell of floor wax. Arriving early in the morning a glimpse of the cleaners could be caught as they put large electric floor polishers away. One of them, named Doris, lived on my street and she was invariably dressed in a light pastel overall coat with pockets stuffed with yellow dusters. The floor-polishing machines looked like lawn mowers except with the rotary blade replaced by a large disc-shaped brush that seemed to glide over the surface of the library's shiny wooden floor. I loved that place: its sense of calm, the stacks filled with books and the sweet smell, as if ideas and dreams were also being polished.

Today public libraries are no longer quite the bastions of silent reflection of yesteryear. Yet they retain the quality of public openness that so many commentators have identified. All too frequently local libraries have been sacrificed on austerity's altar. The New Addington Public Library is one such victim and its revolving door turned for the last time in September 2012. The price of renovating its sixties architecture was deemed too high. Its books have been moved to a smaller space in the newly built New Addington Centre. The shiny new building has retained some of the qualities of the old library. Young people study and contemplate their futures, while elderly women gather to chat and knit. The main difference is that students are not only surrounded by books and notes but installed in front of their laptop computers with mobile phones constantly at their finger tips.

The university library, by contrast, is certainly not open to the world in the same way. A student library card is a necessary visa to gain entry. Having said this, for those who do gain access, many similar pleasures and opportunities are on offer. From the early 1980s the college library at Goldsmiths was a second 'home from home', although I would run back to the New Addington Library during vacation and read all the books I imagined, often misleadingly, that every other student had read already. I have probably spent more hours in Goldsmiths library than in any other. It is an eccentric collection full of gaps and gems. Students are rightly exasperated by the fact that there are not enough copies of essential books in their field. But hidden jewels are there too – it just takes time and assistance to discover them. In this sense, the library is a bit like the university it serves.

Besieged by public spending cuts and subject to so many changes, why do libraries still matter? In the age of Google Scholar, aren't libraries at risk of becoming a bit of an anachronism? Reading matter comes to our screens faster than a book ever could. Why do we need a library when, with the right log-in, we have almost immediate access to the world library online? All this misses the point of libraries because they provide not only a refuge but also places of serendipity, where we discover routinely things we are not looking for.

Tony Woodiwiss has a name for such miracles. He says it is the work of the Library Angel. It is when you discover a book that you didn't know existed and is even more exciting than the one you were trying to find in the first place. Without realizing it the Library Angel has led you there. To meet the Library Angel, or feel her influence, you need to wait for hidden treasures to be revealed. In his famous essay 'Unpacking My Library', Walter Benjamin observes that it is a mistake to think that it is readers that bring books to life. Rather, he argues, the reverse is the case and it is we readers who come to life as our fingers disappear into the pages of a new book.

I used to like to write at night but now know I am at my

best in the mornings. But I often find myself in the library after hours. Scholarship interrupts your sleep. Sometimes – like tonight – there is just no fighting it, nothing left to do other than to get up and get on with the task at hand. With twenty-four-hour and seven-day-a-week library access it is always possible to chase up a new lead or reference. There is a book in the catalogue that I feel sure is the key to the intractable problem preoccupying me on this sleepless night. I am convinced I'll need it when I sit down at the keyboard come morning.

The atmosphere of a library changes at night. In the thick nocturnal silence the library's order is blurred and authority muted. As Alberto Manguel writes, our own thoughts grow louder, and this, he says, is 'halfway between wakefulness and sleep in which the world can comfortably be re-imagined'. The book I am looking for is on the first floor, where the Dewey system offers it an orderly home at 302.231. I find it at the stipulated address. Then something else catches my eye as my fingers stumble along the shelf. It seems more interesting and I grab that book too. My new acquisition is evidence that the Library Angel is still awake. I am ready for the morning now. The heavy stillness of the library at night seems to draw out connections and solutions like a poultice.

The PhD Viva

Today I spoke to a young geographer about his PhD viva. We were having dinner after a political event about racism in Europe and he started to tell me about his thesis defence. 'The best advice my supervisor gave me was to think of the viva not as a threat but an opportunity,' he said. The postgraduate self-help literature describes the viva as an ordeal to be 'survived'.

Traumatic viva tales reinforce the apocalyptic image of what happens in the context of this unusual oral form of examination. All varieties of PhD viva have a basic structure: examiners read the thesis and form an independent judgement about it then ask the candidate questions in the context of 'live talk' which is the literal translation of the Latin phrase viva voce.

The stage in which this live talk takes place varies considerably across the world. In places like Norway and Sweden it is a public affair that takes place in front of academic peers but also friends and family, but in these cases the candidate's performance in the viva has little impact on the outcome. In this sense, the viva is a mock defence and symbolizes the arrival of another intellectual figure in the field and not part of determining whether or not the thesis is to be passed.

201

The PhD Viva

In the UK the event takes place behind closed doors, usually with two examiners – one external to the university and the other internal – sometimes with an academic chairing the discussion and/or with the supervisor present. There is more at stake because the viva is a real examination and can be taken into consideration with regard to the final outcome.

A candidate who has written a good thesis will not fail if they give a poor or even non-existent defence. However, the flaws or weaknesses in a thesis can be mitigated if the candidate offers a robust and eloquent understanding of how they would attend to them. There is a lot to play for in the give and take of the viva, where the author of the thesis comes face to face with two readers who have read it carefully and also have to substantiate their criticisms.

In this sense, the viva for the student is a rare opportunity to talk in detail for one to two hours about their work with two people who have subjected it to a close reading. It would be wrong to minimize what is at stake. My young colleague described the viva as 'a bit like gambling at cards'. What is being played for? The outcome of the viva can vary from a pass without any amendments, to minor corrections that can be made within a few weeks, to a referral in which major corrections are asked for, taking eighteen months and requiring re-examination of the thesis.

In most cases the outcome is minor corrections; extended corrections and unblemished passes are both rare. I have lost track of how many PhD theses I have examined but it must now be over a hundred. In all those projects probably five were passed without any amendments and a similar number were given extended referrals, sometimes not resulting in resubmission.

The viva is far from a foregone conclusion but I think it is some comfort to students anticipating it that the likely outcome is minor corrections detailed in their examiners' joint report stipulating what remains to be done. There is something profound about the metaphor of the viva as a kind of intellectual gambling.

As in a game of poker, you have to be clear about what's in your hand. In a sense, this is about being clear going into the viva, the intellectual cards you have to play. What is of value in your thesis? What is it that other readers in the field will be interested in? What did you find out that surprised you and by extension will surprise others? What is the thesis about and what is its thesis, that is, what is its main argument?

In preparing for the viva it's sometimes as simple as thinking through how to describe in clear and concise terms where the idea for the project came from, how the idea was investigated, what was found out and why it is interesting. Often students worry unnecessarily about being caught out by the examiners referring to an obscure article they haven't read, or by a cringing typographical error that slipped into the submitted thesis. All of these things are of a lesser importance. What is crucial is that the student is clear about what they have in hand, that is, the intellectual, ethical and political integrity of their project and what is to be learnt from it.

The viva has a kind of social etiquette. The examiners read the thesis beforehand, they write independent reports (if they manage their time well), then they meet prior to the viva (often over lunch) and confer and agree key questions to be raised in the viva and a kind of intellectual script designating to each examiner areas of questioning to lead on. The student is very often – almost always in fact – asked an opening question that is designed to get the conversation started. Examples of opening questions range from: 'Tell us where the idea for your project came from?' or 'Reading over your thesis prior to the viva which parts of it were you most proud of and are there any parts of it you would do differently?' Students can anticipate these kinds of questions and it is advisable to prepare or even practise how to answer them.

Some students like to have mock vivas. I am personally not

convinced that they are necessary but what is important is to be prepared to describe in concise but substantive ways the key arguments of the thesis and its main qualities. It is important for students in the context of the viva to take time to reflect and make a considered answer; and to ask for clarification of the question if it isn't clear. Also, allow the examiners to take their time in expressing their reflections and asking their questions.

There is a lot of advice available on postgraduate websites about how to dress, how much to smile, how to flatter the examiners or whether or not to shake hands. These kinds of impression management tactics are usually glaringly obvious and, at least in my experience, completely ineffectual. I think it's better to be yourself and speak sincerely about the things you care about.

The viva is a nerve-racking experience and the most difficult ones I have been involved in have been when the candidate is so nervous that words fail them or where they can't stop themselves talking. Give detailed but brief answers of between two and three minutes. The examiners will want a dialogue, not a lecture. Also, they will want to hear what you have to say (it's important to speak up and speak clearly) but a hectoring diatribe will alienate them.

Continuing the playing card metaphor, students must represent what they think and not fold. Most PhD students fear the question that reveals that their work is based on a false premise and fundamentally flawed, a question that renders them speechless. Often, in preparation for the viva, a student will try to go through the potential questions that might be asked, but it is simply impossible to anticipate all of them. It is possible to prepare how to address or explain to the examiners the weak points in the argument or in the structure of a thesis.

I often think that the best way to approach the examiners' questions is to be both intellectually open to what is raised but at the same time to defend the project's integrity and substance. Sometimes the examiners ask questions that result from misreading and misunderstanding the thesis. I have seen the indignation of an examiner evaporate on more than one occasion when the candidate responds by saying, 'If you look on page 315 I have addressed that issue directly.'

What should a student do if the question exposes a series of issues or consequences that s/he hadn't anticipated or dealt with? The young geographer I mentioned at the beginning described this as the moment when you have to 'decide like playing cards whether to stick or twist'. Sometimes it's better to 'stick' and acknowledge that the incisive question is a good one that will be given further thought. The other option is to 'twist': ask for another card and gamble on opening up the question further, challenging the consequences of the line of critique and the basis of the examiner's judgement.

Part of the art of scholarship is deciding when to accept and learn from a criticism and when to challenge it and elaborate a new argument that extends what you have already written and develops what you want to convey. The viva voce must establish that the thesis is the work of the student, that it has a coherent argument that makes a distinct contribution to knowledge; that it affords evidence of originality and is situated within the relevant literature in relation to the field of study. Keeping these criteria in mind demystifies the viva.

At the end of the viva examiners will more often than not ask students if they have any questions. This can sometimes be very unnerving for students. After that students are asked to leave so that the examiners can confer and decide on the outcome and their recommendation. Once the outcome is known the examiners often discuss and give advice on where the work might be published and possible future directions for the candidate's work.

At its best the viva voce is a live engagement with the ideas of the student. Like the young geographer, some find it, while nerve-racking, an intellectually stimulating and even enjoyable experience. The viva voce should not be a trial by ordeal. However, there are cases when examiners behave badly and these stories fuel postgraduate trepidation about the viva as something to be endured rather than enjoyed. In my experience there have been a handful of occasions when I have witnessed such unprofessional misbehaviour.

I think there are certain kinds of personality types that students and supervisors should avoid inviting to the viva conversation. The first of these is the intellectual narcissist – the kind of examiner who is prone to scour the bibliography for references to their own published work or even ask, '. . . but where am I in the thesis?' Such people can have a distorted self-consciousness about making intellectual judgements: 'What will people think of me if I pass this?' Or, they look at the pages of the thesis as if it were a mirror in which they only see themselves reflected, offering the pretext to go on and on about their own intellectual preoccupations and priorities. The second is the type I would characterize as the time-ruthless academic superstar.

The student's thesis is something to be read at speed and judged – sometimes harshly and unfairly – on the run: 'I only have forty-five minutes for the viva because I have got to catch a plane to my book launch in New York tomorrow.' Many world-renowned and respected academics make fantastic examiners but for others the PhD thesis is a lowbrow read to be perfunctorily scanned.

The last kind of examiner to avoid is the member of the discipline police. Here the concern is usually less about what the thesis has to say than how it can be categorized: 'Is this really sociology?' A PhD student might ask understandably: 'How do I know if the eminent person I want to nominate on my exam entry form falls into one of these categories?' The best indicator of the quality of any given examiner is how they have behaved in previous PhD examinations.

The ideal examiner for a thesis is someone who will read the work in its own terms, be fair and intellectually open-minded and at the same time searching and critical. Probably 90% of all the people I have examined with have demonstrated these qualities.

In the midst of the scaremongering that surrounds the viva voce it is important to realize that the weight of bureaucracy is for once on the student's side: it's much more time-consuming for examiners in terms of paperwork to fail or refer a thesis than it is to pass it. Difficult examiners can be chastened by the realization that their brilliant critical dissection might mean more time will be taken up reading the revised thesis and so keep them away longer from their own work.

Writing and Scholastic Style

Academic writers are often little more than figures of fun. Derided for the opacity of our jargon-filled prose, we swim often unnoticed at the shallow end of the literary pond. To some degree it is our own fault because it seems that to be a serious academic you need to be a seriously bad writer. Anthropologist Brian Morris commented in his inaugural lecture at Goldsmiths in 1999: 'I try to write in a way that is lucid and readable . . . I am continually rebuked for this and told to write in an academic style, that is with pretension and in scholastic jargon, for in academia, obscurantism is equated with intellectual profundity.'

Professor Morris is absolutely right and the mistake that academic authors often make is to confuse 'being clear' with 'simplistic thinking'. There is also a case to be made for the importance of complex writing and dare I say the literary value of academic work. Sometimes difficult and abstract language serves a purpose. The two figures that loom in my mind around this issue are Theodor W. Adorno and George Orwell.

Adorno's prose style is legendary in the opacity stakes. In *Minima Moralia*, my favourite book by him, he makes a strong case for the necessity of difficult writing. 'The logic of the day, which makes so much of its clarity, has naively adopted this perverted notion of everyday speech [. . .] Those who would escape it must recognize the advocates of communicability as traitors to what they communicate.' In Adorno's view the effect of the insistence on communicability results in the betrayal of critical thinking. It is really important to hold to the idea that understanding the world is difficult and can't be served up like a soap opera or the kitsch of reality TV.

Then there is George Orwell's extraordinary essay 'Politics and the English Language'. I try and read it at least once a year. Orwell takes to pieces the language of totalitarian propagandists alongside a critical assessment of the writing of academics of his day like Professor Harold Laski who worked at the London School of Economics. 'If thought corrupts language, language can also corrupt thought. A bad usage can spread by tradition and imitation, even among people who should know better,' wrote Orwell in 1947.

My feeling is that we academic writers need to have both Adorno and Orwell at our elbow as we work. Complex writing is necessary but so too is clarity and the virtues contained in each can be debased. Pristine clarity or abstract complexity is no protection from writing truly awful things.

The miserable plight of the academic writer is not just of our own making. While we are faced with mounting pressure to 'publish or perish', our conditions couldn't be much worse. Some people in fields where the market demand is low literally have to pay to get into print. A friend of mine recently paid £2,000 upfront to get his book out with an academic publisher. He needed to have his book published in order to compete for teaching jobs but no mainstream academic press would take it.

Publishers are making a mint out of academic journals in the so-called science, medical and technical (STM) sector and yet academics receive no payment and, more than this, authors have to sign over their copyright in order to make it into these prestigious tomes. When academic work catches the eye of journalists, or if a TV company needs an 'expert' for their film, there is rarely any thought that there might be some payment for this service. With the exception of the BBC which does pay a fee for broadcast material, commercial media companies view academics as the providers of free insight, regardless of how hard won those insights might be.

Despite all this I don't mind being ridiculed for being an academic writer. It's worth it. Those who champion common sense are more often than not defending a kind of moral cannibalism. There is what Martin Amis calls the 'obscenification of everyday life' in which sensation and exposé fill column inches with salacious reading pleasures.

Equally, there is tabloid prurience that revels in exposing weakness, consuming stars and indulging its readers in what William Hazlitt called the 'pleasures of hating'. We live in a culture where voices are desperately shouting – we speak too quickly before listening. This too is compounded by a fascination with disclosure, confession, revelation. Reading the 'red top' headlines on the train each morning I feel like shouting at the people behind those quivering pages: 'I am an academic, get me out of here.'

Gustav Flaubert wrote: 'I have always tried to live in an ivory tower, but a tide of shit is beating at its walls, threatening to undermine it.' I can't help but feel that not much has changed since he wrote these words in 1872. So, in contrast, the quiet, careful pursuit of obscure things is all the more precious to me. John Berger commented that writers, story tellers, and by extension, academics, are 'death's secretaries'.

I think he meant that writing is about keeping a record and producing a kind of register of life. Here listening with humility might for a moment eclipse the injunction to talk, to narrate, to be noticed. People want to be heard but they don't really want to listen. I think it is within listening that we can find a different kind of ethics, a commitment to democracy and public life. I think this is where academic disciplines, particularly in the social sciences, can play a modest role. The value of academic writing is in the attention it pays to the arcane or otherwise glossed over aspects of life that would otherwise be lost in the cacophony of contemporary culture.

'And What Do You Do
for a Living . . . ?'

I might be alone in this but is anyone else struck rigid with anxiety when asked to explain what we do for a living? The summer holidays are a particularly apprehensive time when it comes to answering this question for those who want to know exactly what we do in universities. Encounters with itinerant Brits holidaying in the sun are among the most excruciating episodes of this kind of status anxiety but weddings or family functions can be just as bad. It's that awful moment when it is time to offer some dinner table account of what being an academic entails.

Usually, I try and fob off such queries and just say that I am a 'teacher'. On one occasion this deflection strategy placed me in hotter water. I was on my way to give a talk at the University of Wolverhampton and running late. I jumped into a minicab at the station and gave the address. The driver asked 'So, what do you do for a living then?' 'I am a teacher,' I replied expecting this answer to satisfy his curiosity. 'I bloody 'ate teachers,' he said, thumping the steering wheel, glancing up at me in the rear view mirror.

He explained how his son had been excluded from school by middle-class idiots who called themselves teachers! I tried to retract the answer. 'Well, actually I am not that kind of teacher . . . I am a university teacher.' The damage was irreparable. Arriving at the Walsall campus he took my money and drove off without making eye contact.

Of course, we are teachers but I suspect that there is something else going on. Being involved in or committed to the 'life of the mind' is still viewed as mildly indecent in England. It's a cliché to say that we live in a thoroughly anti-intellectual culture but I feel its grip tightening. The suspicion of intellectual life is held across social divisions. A friend of my father's used to say that his measure of a person's importance is how useful they'd be if the atom bomb dropped and the world had to be made anew. According to his logic philosophers are dispensable but bricklayers are not.

A not so new vocationalism has become institutionalized through the changes in student finance. Students rightly need to see some return on their investment in university fees and student loans. While pragmatism doesn't completely govern curiosity in our universities, it is a very powerful force. In other ways, the upper middle classes have a longer-standing instrumental approach to education.

A few summers ago I had a few glimpses into this world in the south of France among the British expats in Nice and Cannes. Our neighbours in London, Caroline and Alan, had a curtain-making business but these were not ordinary furnishings and they offered an upmarket service to the rich and famous. They also had a business in the south of France and we often stayed with them there, as they had become surrogate grandparents to our children.

I would sometimes accompany my neighbour Caroline on fitting expeditions and help out in return for their kindness. At some point Caroline would mention to her clients that I was just visiting and the inevitable question would be asked: 'And what do you do for a living?'

'And What Do You Do for a Living . . .?'

One retired accountant who lived in a mansion overlooking the Baie des Anges provides a good case study. His house was like a scene from J.G. Ballard's novel *Supercannes*. At his poolside, bathed in the special glow of the Riviera sun, he decried the then Labour government's aim to increase the numbers of school leavers going into higher education. 'There's no point kids doing degrees that are going to make them unemployable. I read in the *Telegraph* that there are graduates who can't get on training courses to be plumbers.' His other chief target was the profusion of 'Mickey Mouse degrees like media studies and surfing studies'. His sons were studying at redbrick universities 'where they study proper subjects like law and architecture'. When he asked the inevitable question I told him I taught courses in sociology and urban studies and the atmosphere cooled immediately.

My anxiety about these matters might not be unique. There is little self-consciousness about being an intellectual in France but in England it sounds fanciful, affected, or even just plain foolish, to foster such an ambition. Everywhere in public life there is the imperative to consume, to judge value from the point of view of a consumer – 'is this value for money?' Appeals to the importance of understanding as a process, valuable for its own sake, seem very weak in the current climate.

Universities are at their best when they are places where minds are allowed to wander, be it through the labyrinth of high theory or in the lowly task of making the familiar strange. This concern may not be shared but it seems important to stop being afraid of arguing for the vocation of thinking. Anthropologist Clifford Geertz once commented that it was healthy for intellectuals to be made to feel like a fool routinely. He had in mind that this could inhibit the inflation of academic self-importance.

Humility certainly has its uses but this does not mean being shy of arguing for the intellectual life. Critical thinking needs

214

protection from those who would reduce it to a currency traded on the open market of job opportunities. In August every year I take my turn sitting at the clearing desk and interview desperate applicants trying to find a university place. My last question is always what they think education is for. Most mention investing in their future or that a degree will help them get a better job. Every year there is a surprise.

Last summer a young woman came to Goldsmiths for an interview for the BA Sociology course. Her grades were terrible and mostly in science subjects. I asked her my question. 'My parents wanted me to be a doctor and that's why I did all those subjects. I hated them. To me a university degree is for a broader sense of possibilities and for the freedom to make up my own mind about what I want to be interested in.' She got her place. The pragmatists who want to get people back to 'proper trades' and close down 'silly degrees' look past such miracles. Perhaps it is time to be more strident about the value of what we do and to defend the bloodless revolutions in thinking that take place routinely in the seminar room on an almost daily basis.

Primo Levi's House

I live in my house as I live inside my skin: I know more beautiful, more ample, more picturesque skins: but it would seem to me unnatural to change them for mine.

Primo Levi, 'My House' in *Other People's Trades*, 1990

Primo Levi lived in the house he was born in all his life except for his year of enforced exile in Auschwitz. He described himself as an extreme case of a sedentary person, like a family of human molluscs that 'attach themselves to a sea-rock, secrete an outer shell and stay put for the rest of their lives'. It is within the protective shell of Levi's house at Corso Re Umberto 75 in Turin that he wrote *If This Is a Man*, his testimony and analysis of the Nazi death camps. It is here that his life and quest for measured understanding of the most terrible twentieth-century evils ended.

On 11 April 1987 at around 10 a.m. Primo Levi stepped out of Flat 3a onto the third floor landing, pitched himself over the railing and fell to his death. No suicide note was left, no explanation offered. He wrote in his last book that the best defence against death was to focus on 'the aims of life', to busy oneself in palpable everyday tasks. He lost his aim and the shell became a tomb.

Primo Levi worked as an industrial chemist for most of his life, concentrating on his writing after work at the plant was over. He survived the industrial murder of Auschwitz because the regime found a use for his trade. He turned his forensic eye and his literary skill on the regime, becoming perhaps the most brilliant ethnographer of the Nazi terror. His books *The Drowned and the Saved*, *Moments of Reprieve* and *The Truce* documented what he saw and heard from inside the vortex of the Shoah. For Levi, the brilliant evil of Nazism was its ability to make the victims in its own image, to strip them of their humanity. The 'saved' were drawn into what he called the 'zone of grey consciences', summed up in the acts of compromise and compliance that became the price of survival. Many survivors paid for this later, Levi wrote, when they abandoned hope and took their own lives.

The circumstances of Primo Levi's death are much contested and pored over. In the immediate aftermath of his death *The New Yorker* published an editorial claiming Levi had cheated his readers through taking his own life. Others like Diego Gambetta maintain that he did not commit suicide; it had been a terrible accident.

The publication of two biographies in 2002 reinvigorated the controversy. Between them, these books – by Carole Angier and Ian Thomson, respectively – amount to over 1,500 pages of conjecture on the true nature of Primo Levi as a man. The only good sentences in these books are there by proxy. They are there in the citations, the epigrams, in the voice of Primo Levi himself.

It is perhaps the same puzzle and the mystery of Levi's death that took me to Turin in search of something. I am not sure what that something is, or was, even now. But I know that there is, or should be, a line past which curiosity should not go. The problem is that one is often aware of that line only at the point that it has been overstepped. What follows is perhaps a

cautionary tale or, looked at another way, a posthumous lesson from the twentieth-century's greatest witness.

It's a hot August day. The long drive from Nice has taken
almost six hours. Turin at 1 p.m. is almost completely desert-
ed. The Fiat factory is closed for its annual holiday and everyone has left town to holiday on the Riviera. My wife and three
children have made the long drive with me, sacrificing a day
on the beach.

After some quick advice from a taxi driver we find our
way to Corso Re Umberto. The first thing that is immediately
striking is the horse chestnut trees that line the street. There
it is, number 75, the building immediately recognizable from
the photograph in Carole Angier's biography. The building is
early twentieth century, made of red brick with a grey stone
façade at street level.

This district to the west of the city is called Crocetta ('Little
Cross'), a middle-class district that has seen better times. We
park and the children get out and play in the empty street. As
I walk towards the dark wooden door there is a list of names
on a brass plate; among them is written the name 'Levi'.

Two women brush past my shoulder to open the door and
I follow in behind them. The external plainness of the building
gives way to a turn-of-the-century elegance. The internal court-
yard opens to the sky and has white walls. A few paces to the
right and another door and my chest tightens. There is the foot
of the staircase and the mosaic floor where Primo Levi fell.

The staircase coils upwards like a misshapen spring. A lift
rises up through the centre and the box and pulley structure
looks like an angular steel arachnid. The concierge, a small,
friendly, Latin American man, comes out to ask me something. I try to explain but he doesn't understand. I start to
climb the stairs and he waves his arms: 'Signora Levi,' he says
pointing upstairs. Signora Levi is home? He runs up to the first
floor to see if there is anyone who can interpret.

A middle-aged, bespectacled, bald man comes out of the offices of a sun bed company located upstairs. I explain that I am an admirer of Primo Levi's writing and that I have come here as a kind of pilgrimage. He explains that Primo Levi's wife, Anna Maria Levi, along with her son, Renzo, live in the building. He signals three with one hand while holding his other hand flat just above his hip. 'With three children?' I ask. 'Yes, three children,' he replies. I ask him if I can walk up the stairs. The concierge looks nervous. The middle-aged man speaks to him in Italian. The concierge shrugs and gestures with an upturned palm toward the staircase. 'You are not to disturb Signora Levi,' he says in broken English.

The cold stone stairs have slight curves worn smooth by the many feet that have climbed them. The clanking sounds of the steel lift echo around the walls. By the time I reach the third floor the concierge is waiting for me. He shows me the door and there to the right of the door, next to the bell is a small plate with the name 'Renzo Levi'. As a reflex I reach out and touch it. The concierge points to an adjacent door with number 10 on it.

The door is large, dark wood, tanned by time. He indicates that the family occupies the whole floor. I look up and there is a window open, possibly a bathroom or a kitchen. I turn towards the banister and look down. The tightness in my chest increases. The concierge gestures with his hands that this is where Primo Levi dived over the edge. It is a fall of at least 60 feet.

The banister is high, too high to have tumbled over by accident even for a tall man, which Primo Levi was not. The view is terrifying. Saul Bellow once commented that death is like the dark side of the mirror, impenetrable but at the same time necessary. I look down once more. The chilling drop is like the dark side of the mirror, nothing beyond it, nothing reflected back.

'My God,' I hear myself say. The tightness in my chest moves to my stomach. I don't remember walking down the stairs. The concierge is less anxious now. He points to the area next to the lift. While the fall smashed Levi's skull and broke most of his bones, his face remained unmarked. The concierge sees my old-fashioned camera on my wrist and mimes taking a photograph. I take the camera and in a split second the picture is taken.

I am suddenly awake to the shameful intrusion crossing the line between homage and voyeurism. Perhaps I had crossed it before the shutter clicked. Walking back to the entrance I pass a man without seeing his face. The concierge stops and bows his head slightly. The man disappears up the stairs. I turn to leave but the concierge signals me to stop and wait. He holds his index finger to his lips. We pass through the grand wooden door onto the steps of Corso Re Umberto 75. 'E il figlio,' he says. Figlio? Son? Was that Primo Levi's son Renzo, I ask? 'Si . . . si, Renzo.'

Outside, I wander around the house slightly dazed, not quite believing what happened. I watch my own three children play among the horse chestnut trees by the road. Looking up at the third floor balcony I imagine Primo Levi throwing money wrapped in paper to pedlars and beggars below.

'Did you find him, Dad?' asks one of my daughters as we get in the car. 'No, love, no I didn't.' Leaving Turin we head for the coast and begin the long drive back to Nice. She was right – I guess I had been looking for Primo Levi. There was no sign of him, just the shape of the life he had left behind – his son, the three grandchildren he had never known and his wife. I had been an intruder in the world that he left behind.

It made me think again about his recent biographers' attempts to divine the inner working of his thoughts, the nature of his sexuality, the quality of his marriage, not least the attempts of those who have written about him to know what was in his mind when he walked out onto the third floor landing before falling to his death.

In the republic of letters biographers are the body snatchers. I guess I had always wanted to believe that his death was an accident. Perhaps, that is what I was here for. I had become a body snatcher too. Standing there looking down from his last vantage point convinces me of the error of that hope. Primo Levi always insisted on the injunction to communicate. His writing was his attempt to hold up a mirror to the world and to himself. That is where I should be looking for him, in his books, and not some backstreet in Turin.

For a long time I did not know what to do with the camera film I had used that day. It remained in the camera for months, hiding the illicit and shameful cargo. It was autumn by the time the film returned from being developed. I opened the package and saw – blank, all blank, the dark side of the mirror.

Lost Notebook

In his essay 'The Writer on Holiday', Roland Barthes suggests that there is a cunning mystification contained in good-natured summer portrayals of literary figures taking time off. The authors in question cannot conform to 'factory time', they simply continue with their vocation while on vacation. 'Writers are on holiday, but their Muse is awake, and gives birth non-stop.' Barthes' aim is to decode societal myths: 'By having holidays, he displays the sign of his being human; but the god remains, one is a writer as Louis XIV was a king, even on the commode.' The work of writers sets them apart as literary gods and yet at the same time the holiday snaps make them prosaic. Barthes captures something profound about the inability to 'switch off' or take a holiday from the life of the mind. Even standing in the line for a ride at Disneyland we sociologists are still making mental 'field notes'.

How many of us – graduate students and professors alike – sneak books and notebooks into our hand luggage? 'I'll just take some work with me . . . in case I get time.' I am as guilty as anyone else. This brings dangers and risks far beyond simply trying the patience of our nearest and dearest. A few years ago I took the ferry from Portsmouth to Bilbao with my wife and children, en route to the coast of northern Spain. Staying there overnight we visited the Guggenheim Museum. The curved steel structure looked like some vast ship-like crab that had crawled up out of the sea.

The shining building contained not a single straight line in its structure. At the time a retrospective of artist Juan Muñoz was showing. Muñoz studied at Croydon Art College and spent many of his artistically formative years in London. He died in 2001 at the young age of 48. Credited with re-introducing human figures to modern sculpture, many of his works have a sociological quality concerned with listening, incommensurability, how the familiar remains a mystery. The exhibition was a 'sociologist's holiday'. My family left me to it, wandering for probably far too long through the astonishing collection of paintings, sculptures, sound and video installations. I was so taken with it, I returned the next day to watch once more a play that Muñoz had written with John Berger called 'Will It Be a Likeness?'

My family took a bearing for the shops as I headed off towards the museum one last time. Armed with a huge bag of change I waited in line. When it was my turn I produced the jingling bag and asked the woman behind the desk to forgive me. She helped me count the money and as we got to the last pile of copper coins (the entrance fee was 12.50 euros), my eldest daughter came charging into the museum in floods of tears. 'Dad, come quick – our car has been broken into.' We ran back to the car park.

The rear windows were smashed and a bag – containing all my wife's and my clothes – was missing. Incandescent with rage, my wife mentally ran her fingers through the wardrobe of clothes in the stolen bag: a swimsuit bought for the holiday, a multicoloured skirt purchased several years before in Spain, her 'special' blouse. She couldn't comprehend why I seemed matter of fact about the theft. 'I don't understand you,'

she said tearfully in exasperation. 'You don't seem to be bothered or upset.'

The truth is I wasn't really bothered by the larceny, even
though we had to confront the prospect of surviving the next
two weeks in the clothes we were standing up in. I tried to comfort my daughter – her art book, paints and crayons had also
been taken. I told her that you have to try and keep vicious
and violent things from touching you deeply. She couldn't understand why I wasn't angry either and my words were of little
consolation.

After an hour a police officer dressed in plain clothes – a
detective – arrived. He asked me to follow him to the station.
Arriving there, he invited me into an office where I tried to
explain the incident in my pidgin Spanish. His English was
predictably better. He told me that he'd visited Britain regularly. He had a relative who lived in 'Royal Tunbridge Wells'
and the aristocratic connection of the country town seemed
important to him. I explained that I would need a report written in English for insurance purposes. He started to write but
he struggled to find the right words. I offered to do it for him;
I explained that I was an academic. 'Oh, so you write books,
eh?' I said I did. 'Sure,' he said ushering me in front of the
computer screen. I started to type with the detective interject-
ing enthusiastically.

'The being of the person who is stole . . . What is that?'
'The victim,' I replied.
'Ah, si – the victeeem,' he repeated.
'The bag of the victeem,' he said, apparently pleased with his
newfound command of English.

After about thirty minutes the report was written. It was actually a very pleasant experience of co-authorship. As I left, the
detective opened his palms and shrugged his shoulders.

'I am sooorry,' he said.

After what seemed like a long pause, he continued: 'I hope your holiday will be better. Perhaps, you will make a book about this?'

'Perhaps,' I replied, as we shook hands.

The shattered glass cleaned out of the car, I returned to my family and found them outside the Guggenheim Museum tucking into ice creams.

It wasn't until a few days later that I realized that stowed away secretly in that stolen bag was . . . a notebook. It was almost completely full of scribbled ideas, references and intellectual 'notes to self'. It was only then that I started to think about the value of what had been lost. As I tried to remember what it contained, my stomach tightened as I calculated the full extent of the nauseating loss. The clothes hadn't mattered to me, it was easy to brush that off, but a beloved Moleskine full of reflections written over a period of six months? What price on that?

If 'the pen is the tongue of the mind' as Miguel de Cervantes commented, then the notebook is its ledger. The notebook contained a record of leads, faithfully copied quotations, an ethnographic compendium of overheard conversations, answers to matters of fact, lists of bibliographic leads. The notebook is the fundamental tool of the trade, the mind's imprint on paper. What had been stolen was in fact irreplaceable. It was thinking time, something that can be, at best, only partially recalled. I strained to remember but also mourned the loss of what I could not.

Thinking about it now, I often don't go back to the notebooks once they are full. There is comfort in knowing that those preliminary thoughts are there though, if ever needed.

Lost Notebook

In the case of the stolen notebook, however, it was full of extended notes, information and even passages written out in longhand that I planned to publish. A few days after our ordeal in Bilbao, and still bemoaning the loss of the pilfered notebook, my daughter said, in answer to yet another of my complaints about the theft: 'The thing about notebooks, Dad . . . you can't back them up, can you?' She's right of course but you can leave them at home! Packing for the annual vacation, now only novels make it into the luggage, no space for smuggled notebooks or things to do 'if I just get a spare moment'.

Afterword:
How the Diary Came to Be Written
in the First Place

The idea for this book had a long gestation period. It all started in 2003 when I was asked to write a regular column for the university teachers' union magazine, which at the time was called *AUTlook*. Initially, to write something of interest to academics across the range of disciplines on a regular basis was a real challenge. I loved the idea of being a columnist, with all its journalistic grandeur, even though the cartoon portrait of me produced by the magazine gave my friends ceaseless opportunities to tease me. Puzzled by the unrecognizable face, my son said when he saw the cartoon for the first time, 'Who is that mixed-race man, Daddy?'

After a while I stumbled on a method of producing the regular column by drawing on my anthropological training. In her book *Killing Thinking* Mary Evans writes: 'Academic life has become subject to a degree of bureaucratic control which needs urgent anthropological investigation as a new form of social life and universities would repay the investigation of trained ethnographers.' I began keeping a 'field diary', although one with a somewhat broader focus than is outlined here. Each column would begin with a small incident that had actually happened and a larger argument would be drawn out from it about current issues relating to the life of the university. Some of those columns – albeit revised and updated – are included in this book. After several years of writing this column the idea dawned on me that there might be a book in it, albeit an unconventional one.

Initially, I took the idea to a range of publishers. Academic publishing is constrained by its own formats, usually concerned with student-orientated books or practical handbooks that will secure high sales, although people who work in publishing are, in my experience, very often book lovers. There was a lot of interest, and even excitement, but the idea simply didn't fit. 'Could you write like an academic self-help book?' one publisher commented, or, 'Maybe you should write a book about how to be a professor before you are 40.' All this advice was given in good faith but I had little or no interest in following it. I wrote a book proposal which was turned down after getting mixed reviews.

For some considerable time I felt defeated and resigned to the fact that this was an idea that would never be realized. It wasn't until I met Kat Jungnickel who suggested an online format that it came back to life. Kat has a PhD in sociology but she is also a filmmaker and a professional digital designer. She immediately understood the idea and could envision the project. Kat embodies the intellectual virtues of curiosity, openness, dynamism and creativity that I have tried to argue for in this book and I am eternally grateful for her generosity. In 2011 it was made available online through Kat's inventiveness and the help of Caedmon Mullin at Big Pebbles Media (http://www.academic-diary.co.uk). The response to it was amazing. One of the advantages of online publishing is that you can see who is reading it and it became clear that tens of thousands of people have accessed it from all over the world.

I always wanted the diary to be a book that you could hold and flick through. When Sarah Kember approached me with the idea of publishing the diary as the first publication of Goldsmiths Press I jumped at the chance. This book includes many more new entries than the online version and the older ones have been updated. It is particularly appropriate for this to be published by Goldsmiths Press because, as you will have appreciated by now, this is not a conventional academic book and it is set largely in an unconventional academic place.

I have tried to write with as much honesty as I can muster, reflecting on my failings and mistakes as well as actions and judgements I'd stand by. Many of the diary entries were written in 'down time', during holidays, in the cracks of the day and sometimes late at night. The entries are short because I imagine that you will read them in a similar way, in transit, or in a calm moment over a cup of tea or coffee, squeezed in between the gaps of more pressing commitments. They are so many silent conversations with myself about how to live a good life in the university. The last entries were completed during the Christmas holidays in 2014. While I have tried to be candid, I am mindful that ultimately, like everyone else, I too am a stranger to myself. By now you – the reader – will have decided whether or not this experiment in writing differently is successful.

Before closing the diary's pages I would like to thank Pat Loughrey, Roger Burrows, Sarah Kember and Adrian Driscoll for believing in the idea of a book-length version of it. Thanks to Roberto Feo and Stuart Bannocks for all their excellent work on the design of this book and also to Ben Craggs for steering the project to its final completion. Also, sincere thanks to Kat Jungnickel and Caedmon Mullins for helping realize the first online stage of the project. I'd also like to thank Judith Barrett and Jane Offerman for editing and correcting the liberties I too often take with the English language. Thanks to friends and colleagues who encouraged me to pursue this idea, even when I should have been spending my time in more academically gainful ways. In the category a special mention is deserved for Avery Gordon, Anamik Saha, Stephen Dobson, David Yewman, Yasmin Gunaratnam, Nirmal Puwar, Mariam Motamedi-Fraser, Nick Gane, David Beer, Pat Thomson and Fran Tonkiss. I also need to thank my teachers, students – past and present – and colleagues at Goldsmiths with whom I have shared so much – so special thanks to Pat Caplan, Nici Nelson, Brian Morris, John Solomos, Parminder Bhachu, Paul Gilroy, Vron Ware, Joe Baden, Simon Williams, Neil Bradley, Chloe Nast, Violet Fearon, Lauren Mehr, Lauren O'Donnell, Mary Claire Halvorson, Lesley Hewings, Carole Bird, Sarah Reed, Bev Skeggs, Noortje Marres, Beckie Coleman, Alex Rhys-Taylor, Lez Henry, Mónica Moreno Figueroa, Colin King, Yasmeen Narayan, Emma Jackson, Hiroki Ogasawara, Takeshi Arimoto, Charlotte Bates, Brett St Louis, Michaela Benson, Vik Loveday, Miranda Iossifidis, Aisha Phoenix, Anna Bull, Phil Thomas, Delphine and Sim Colton, Vic Seidler, Flemming Røgilds, and last but not least 'Mr Goldsmiths', Trevor Blair.

Our loved ones and family are the true witnesses to our academic obsessions. They know the true shape of our embarrassment. I need to thank my family for their patience and forgiveness, particularly my wife Debbie, who I kept waiting too many times while off pursuing intellectual distractions and preoccupations! I hope now I am a more reformed character. Also, thanks to my children – Stevie, Sophie and Charlie – all of whom have grown up around the clutter of papers and books, as well as the pressures and scandals of academic life. As you will have read, they appear intermittently through these pages, often as voices of reason and grounding sentiments that bring me back down to earth. I need to thank them for offering those bearings as well as the many other ordinary miracles that are too numerous to name, including tolerating my crazy summer digressions and pilgrimages. Perhaps the trips to Hawaii, Austin and Gothenberg compensate partially for all the madness. I hope that reading the diary will explain why higher education matters so much to me and what I felt was at stake when I left home each morning for the first appointment of the day.

Tips, Leads and Follow-Ups

The process of turning the diary into a book raised a practical question: how should I reference the literature cited and the ideas of the writers who had influenced it? Would I use the conventional styles of academic referencing and/or include footnotes? Trying to make the diary fit a conventional academic style just seemed counter to the spirit of this experiment in writing differently.

Citation is the academic equivalent of good manners and referencing the work and ideas that influence our thinking is a matter of giving credit where credit is due. As you will have read, authors are mentioned and cited throughout the diary. All of that work is detailed below. Rather than merely compile a standard bibliography I have grouped the work that I have used under a number of themes. The intention here is that the annotations will provide a guide to reading tips and ideas to follow up that include books but also blogs and online resources.

Tips, Leads and Follow-Ups

Universities in Changing Times

There is a very lively and insightful critical literature on how public universities have been transformed by commercialization and the education consequences of these changing financial pressures around funding. Authors like Marina Warner and Rosalind Gill have vividly documented the corrosive affects this has for faculty and scholars from within the university. There is also an abundance of analysis of how these transformations are changing the role of the university and its relationship to society more broadly (see Evans, Collini, McGettigan, Readings, Newfield). Among these, Roger Burrows and Derek Sayer have written excellent critiques of the consequences and hypocrisies that result as metrics have proliferated to rank and judge academic value for individuals, departments and universities.

In addition, there is important new critical writing on how academic authority is colonized by white somatic norms in the university and how class, race and gender inequalities structure the academy. Sara Ahmed deconstructs these forms of power and the racialized expectations that follow from them and shows how new knowledges are produced out of a struggle to achieve real change. Also, Yasmin Gunaratnam describes the consequences this has for black feminist scholars who, as a result of the racialized expectations placed upon them, are experiencing what she calls 'presentation fever'. Nathan Richard's important films *Absent from the Academy* and *Why is My Curriculum So White?* document both the underrepresentation of people of colour inside the universities and the enduring Eurocentric nature of the curriculum.

I have listed a range of the writing I have found most useful in making sense of what is happening to the university in uncertain and changing times.

236

Ahmed, Sara. (2012) *On Being Included: Racism and Diversity in Institutional Life.* Durham, NC and London: Duke University Press.

Bailey, Michael. (2015) 'The Strange Death of the Liberal University', 3 April, *Opendemocracy*, https://www.opendemocracy.net/michael-bailey/strange-death-of-liberal-university

Bate, Jonathan, ed. (2011) *The Public Value of the Humanities.* London: Bloomsbury Academic.

British Sociological Society Sociology and the Cuts blog, available at: http://sociologyandthecuts.wordpress.com/

Burrows, R. (2012) 'Living with the H-Index Metric Assemblages in the Contemporary Academy', *The Sociological Review*, 60(2): 355–372.

Campaign For the Public University Campaign for the Public University, website available at: http://publicuniversity.org.uk

Collini, Stefan. (2012) *What are Universities For?* London: Penguin Books.

Collini, Stefan. (2013) 'Sold Out', *London Review of Books*, 35(20) (24 October): 3–12.

Evans, Mary. (2004) *Killing Thinking: the Death of the Universities.* London: Continuum.

Gill, Rosalind. (2010) 'Secrets, Silences and Toxic Shame in the Neoliberal University', in Róisín Ryan-Flood and Rosalind Gill, eds. *Secrecy and Silence in the Research Process: Feminist Reflections.* London: Routledge, pp. 228–245.

Tips, Leads and Follow-Ups

Gunaratnam, Yasmin. (2015) 'Presentation Fever and Podium Affects', *Case-Stories*, 18 March, available at: http://www.case-stories.org/blog/2015/3/8/presentation-fever

Harney, Stefano and Moten, Fred. (2013) *The Undercommons: Fugitive Planning & Black Study*. Brooklyn, NY: Autonomedia.

Kelly, Aidan and Burrows, Roger. (2012) 'Measuring the Value of Sociology? Some Notes on the Performative Metricisation of the Contemporary Academy', in Lisa Adkins and Celia Lury, eds. *Measure and Value: A Sociological Review Monograph*. Oxford: Wiley-Blackwell, pp. 130–150.

Kerr, Clark. (1963) *The Idea of the University*. Cambridge, MA: Harvard University Press.

Knowles, Caroline and Burrows, Roger. (2014) 'The Impact of Impact', *Etnográfica*, 18(2): 237–254.

McGettigan, Andrew. (2013) *The Great University Gamble: Money, Markets and the Future of Higher Education*. London: Pluto Press.

Newfield, Christopher. (2008) *Unmaking the Public University: the Forty-year Assault on the Middle Class*. Cambridge, MA: Harvard University Press.

Readings, Bill. (1996) *The University in Ruins*. Cambridge, MA: Harvard University Press.

Remaking the University – Michael Meranze and Christopher Newfield's blog, available at: http://utotherescue.blogspot.co.uk

Richards, Nathan E., dir. (2013) *Absent From the Academy*. London: A Narrative Media, available at: https://vimeo.com/76725812

Richards, Nathan E., dir. (2014) *Why is My Curriculum So White?* London: A Narrative Media.

Sayer, Derek. (2014) *Rank Hypocrisies: The Insult of the REF*. London: Sage.

Taylor, Laurie. (2012) 'What's Wrong with University?', *New Humanist*, March/April, pp. 34–37.

Warner, Marina. (2014) 'Diary: Why I Quit', *The London Review of Books*, 36(17): 42–43.

Warner, Marina. (2015) 'Learning My Lesson', *The London Review of Books*, 37(6): 8–14.

Tips, Leads and Follow-Ups

Campus fictions

Elaine Showalter commented that campus novels are valuable because they offer a kind of social barometer of university life. I think she is right. I cited her study of campus novels in the opening sections of this book. I have also included a list of some of my favourite books. Ann Oakley, a sociologist and novelist, commented that the main purpose of a campus novel is to amuse. 'Academic pomposity must laugh at itself, or we are all definitely doomed.' The satire often contains serious insight. For example, re-reading Frank Parkin's campus farce *The Mind and Body Shop* it is striking how many things that seemed like harmless artistic licence in 1987 have actually become realities (i.e. the loss of university pensions, commercialization of the university, rampant managerialism).

Campus fiction also captures some of the hidden social damage and tragedy in great minds humbled by time. Philip Roth's novel *The Human Stain* captures the complex drama of racism in America through the fate of his protagonist Coleman Silk. Silk sacrificed his African American family and past to pass as a white and become a professor of classics. Then Silk loses his job as a consequence of an accusation of racism being made against him. Lisa Genova's novel *Still Alice* tells of a Harvard psychology professor – Alice Hoffman – who is stripped of all the academic things she holds dear by early onset Alzheimer's disease, the first sign of which is when she stares blankly at an article, unable to complete a peer review for the *Journal of Cognitive Psychology*.

Academic fictions often find a way to speak about the inaudible tensions and anxieties in academic life. Zadie Smith's novel *On Beauty* is a cautionary tale of an art professor, Howard Belsey, whose critical imagination blocks him from seeing any beauty in art. It is also a study of how academic life carries a cost for his long-suffering wife Kikki. Theirs is a 'mixed mar-

240

riage' – I am not referring to the fact it is a union of an African American woman and a white Englishman. Rather, Smith captures brilliantly the position of non-academic partners in her dinner party descriptions. Kikki is constantly questioning herself because she cannot quite read the in-jokes, the academic references to Foucault or Derrida, or the allusions to disciplinary infighting or adoration.

I have assembled some of my favourite campus novels in the list below along with a couple of critical studies of the genre.

Bradbury, Malcolm. (1975) *The History Man*.
London: Penguin Books.

Carter, Ian. (1990) *Ancient Cultures of Conceit: British University Fiction in the Post-War Years*. London: Routledge.

Genova, Lisa. (2007) *Still Alice*. London: Simon and Schuster.

Lodge, David. (1978) *Changing Places: A Tale of Two Campuses*.
London: Penguin Books.

Lodge, David. (1984) *Small World*.
London: Secker and Warburg.

Lodge, David. (1989) *Nice Work*.
London and New York: Penguin Books.

McCarthy, Mary. (1951) *The Groves of Academe*.
New York: Harcourt.

McGuire, Ian. (2007) *Incredible Bodies*.
London: Bloomsbury Publishing.

Oakley, Ann. (1988) *The Men's Room*. London: Virago.

Oakley, Ann. (1999) *Overheads*. London: HarperCollins.

Parkin, Frank. (1987) *The Mind and Body Shop*.
New York: Atheneum.

Russo, Richard. (1997) *Straight Man*.
New York: Random House.

Showalter, E. (2005) *Faculty Towers: The Academic Novel and its Discontents*. Oxford: Oxford University Press.

Smiley, Jane. (1995) *Moo*. New York: Alfred A. Knopf.

Smith, Zadie. (2005) *On Beauty: A Novel*.
London: Penguin Books.

Tartt, Donna. (1992) *A Secret History*.
New York: Alfred A. Knopf.

Students, learning and teaching

Included here are a range of texts that reflect on pedagogy and teaching. They are not conventional 'how to' guides on writing 'learning objectives' and preferred styles of lecturing. Rather, they focus on the ethics and politics of teaching itself and range from bell hooks' extraordinary books on learning and transgression to Mitch Albom's tribute to his sociology teacher Morrie Schwartz. I have also included some references on teaching, race and difference and the importance of addressing issues of power in the classroom (particularly Bhattacharyya), as well as the relationship between teaching and intellectual generosity (see Roman and Coles).

Richard Hoggart's memoir listed here also demonstrates the central role of teaching in writing. As an extra-mural evening teacher in Hull in the 1950s Hoggart was free during the day to write his classic *The Uses of Literacy*. It was also true for Raymond Williams and E.P. Thompson who wrote their early books while teaching at night. For each of them teaching provided a way to test and try out their ideas. This serves as a reminder that students are after all our first public and our main audience.

There are also references here to the new opportunities of using mass online teaching platforms or MOOCs. Here there is both the potential to reach wider audiences but, at the same time, as Marc Parry points out, MOOCs are also being used to replace actual teachers in the classroom and as a way to enable educational cutbacks on staffing. I have also included two books on how to be a more compelling public speaker by David Yewman and his co-author Andy Craig. These guides are crammed with tips and good ideas that are applicable when giving a first-year undergraduate lecture or a conference keynote.

Tips, Leads and Follow-Ups

Albom, Mitch. (1997) *Tuesdays with Morrie: an Old Man and Young Man and Life's Great Lesson*. New York: Doubleday.

Bhattacharyya, Gargi. (1999) 'Teaching Race in Cultural Studies: a Ten-step Programme of Personal Development', in John Solomos and Martin Bulmer, eds. *Ethnic and Racial Studies Today*. London: Routledge, pp. 73–84.

Callender, Claire and Jackson, Jonathan. (2005) 'Does the Fear of Debt Deter Students from Higher Education?', *Journal of Social Policy*, 34: 509–540.

Craig, Andy and Yewman, David. (2014) *Weekend Language: Presenting with More Stories and Less Powerpoint*. Vancouver and Washington, DC: Elevatorspeech.

Coles, Romand. (1997) *Rethinking Generosity: Critical Theory and the Politics of Caritas*.
Ithaca, NY: Cornell University Press.

Dewey, John. (1910) *How We Think*. Boston, MA: D.C. Heath.

Dobson, Stephen. (2006) 'The Assessment of Student PowerPoint Presentations – Attempting the Impossible?', *Assessment & Evaluation in Higher Education*, 31(1): 109–119.

Hoggart, Richard. (1991) *A Sort of Clowning – Life and Times*: 1940–1959. Oxford: Oxford University Press.

hooks, bell. (2003) *Teaching Community: A Pedagogy of Hope*. New York: Routledge.

hooks, bell. (1994) *Teaching to Transgress: Education as the Practice of Freedom*. New York: Routledge.

244

Nietzsche, Friedrich. (1909) *On the Future of Our Educational Institutions: Homer and Classical Philology.*
London: George Allen & Unwin.

Parry, Marc. (2013) 'A Star MOOC Professor Defects – at Least for Now', *The Chronicle of Higher Education*, 3 September, http://chronicle.com/article/A-MOOC-Star-Defects-at-Least/141331/

Roman, Leslie G. (2015) 'Making and Moving Publics: Stuart Hall's Projects, Maximal Selves and Education', *Discourse: Studies in the Cultural Politics of Education*, 36(2): 200–226, DOI: 10.1080/01596306.2015.1014225.

Yewman, David. (2007) *On Getting to the Point.*
Vancouver and Washington, DC: DASH Consulting, Inc.

Tips, Leads and Follow-Ups

On writing and writers

Collected here are some of the best sources for writing tips that I have found. Some of them focus on the practicalities, discipline and rituals of writing (Becker, King, Eco, Curry, Silvia), while others reflect on the physicality of writing and the tools of the trade (Barthes, Ingold, Gordon, Krementz). One of the central debates in this literature is between those who argue for the intellectual value of complex theoretical language (Adorno, Miller) as opposed to others who advocate for clarity in prose style (Orwell, Billig, Morris).

Sarah Kember and John Holmwood reflect on what is happening to writing in the changing digital environment, particularly focusing on the issue of making it available via open access. They question whether this is necessarily a progressive development and point to the financial limitations that are likely to restrict open access publishing. Sarah Kember's work also offers a deep reflection on the possibilities of new forms of writing, as well as the confinements placed on academic authors today.

Adorno, Theodor. (1978) *Minima Moralia*. London: Verso.

Authors' Licensing & Collecting Society. ALCS website http://www.alcs.co.uk

Back, Les. (2007) *The Art of Listening*. Oxford: Berg.

Barthes, Roland. (1973) 'The Writer on Holiday', in *Mythologies*. London: Granada, pp. 29–31.

Barthes, Roland. (2010) 'An Almost Obsessive Relation to Writing Implements [1973]' in *The Grain of the Voice: Interviews 1962–1980*. London: Vintage Books, pp. 177–182., IL

Becker, Howard S. (1998) *Tricks of the Trade: How to Think About Your Research While You're Doing It.* Chicago, IL and London: University of Chicago Press.

Becker, Howard S. (2007) *Telling About Society.* Chicago, IL and London: University of Chicago Press.

Billig, Michael. (2013) *Learn to Write Badly: How to Succeed in the Social Sciences.* Cambridge: Cambridge University Press.

Curry, Mason. (2013) *Daily Rituals: How Great Minds Make Time, Find Inspiration, and Get to Work.* London: Picador.

Eco, Umberto. (2015) *How to Write a Thesis.* Cambridge, MA: MIT Press.

Geertz, Clifford. (1988) *Works and Lives: the Anthropologist as Author.* London: Polity Press.

Gordon, Mary. (1999) 'Putting Pen to Paper, but Not Just Any Pen or Just Any Paper', *The New York Times*, 5 July, http://partners.nytimes.com/library/books/070599gordon-writing.html

Holmwood, John. (2013a) 'Commercial Enclosure. Whatever Happened to Open Access?', *Radical Philosophy*, 181: 2–5.

Holmwood, John. (2013b) 'Markets versus Dialogue: The Debate over Open Access Ignores Competing Philosophies of Openness', *London School of Economics Impact of Social Sciences*, 21 October, available at: http://blogs.lse.ac.uk/impactofsocialsciences/2013/10/21/markets-versus-dialogue/

Ingold, Tim. (2012) 'In Defence of Handwriting', *Writing Across Borders – Writing on Writing, Department of Anthropology*, University of Durham, https://www.dur.ac.uk/writingacrossboundaries/writingonwriting/timingold/

Kember, Sarah. (2014) 'Why Write? Feminism, Publishing and the Politics of Communication', *New Formations*, 83: 99–117.

Kember, Sarah and Zylinska, Joanna. (2012) *Life After New Media. Mediation as a Vital Process.* Cambridge, MA and London: MIT Press.

King, Stephen. (2001) *On Writing: A Memoir of the Craft.* London: New English Library.

Krementz, Jill. (1996) *The Writer's Desk.* New York: Random House.

Lepenies, Wolf. (1988) *Between Literature and Science: the Rise of Sociology.* Cambridge: Cambridge University Press.

Miller, James. (2000) 'Is Bad Writing Necessary: George Orwell, Theodor, and the Politics of Language', *Linguafranca: The Review of Academic Life*, December/January, pp. 33–44.

Morris, Brian. (1995) 'How to Publish a Book and Gain Recognition as an Academic', *Anthropology Today*, 11(1): 15–17.

Orwell, George. (1968b) 'Politics and the English Language', in *The Collected Essays, Journalism and Letters: Volume 4.* London: Penguin Books, pp. 156–169.

Perec, Georges. (2009) 'Notes on the Objects to be Found on My Desk', in *Thoughts of Sorts*.
Boston, MA: A Verba Mundi Book, pp. 11–16.

Rushdie, Salman. (1991) 'Is Nothing Sacred?',
in *Imaginary Homelands: Essays and Criticism 1981–1991*.
London: Penguin, pp. 416–429.

Silvia, Paul J. (2007) *How to Write A Lot: A Practical Guide to Productive Academic Writing*.
Washington, DC: American Psychological Association.

Welty, Eudora. (1995) *One Writer's Beginnings*.
Cambridge, MA: Harvard University Press.

Tips, Leads and Follow-Ups

Intellectual life and its purpose

The fundamental tool of our trade is reading. Included here are references to Alberto Manguel's insightful books, some on the history and times of reading. Also included is Walter Benjamin's classic essay on unpacking his library and the relationship between the reader and his or her book collection. Homi Bhahba's retelling of the scene of unpacking brings some of the issues around academic reading up to date.

Some of the references included here reflect on daily realities and routines of intellectual life, like Pat Thomson's wonderful blog *Patter* and Zygmunt Bauman's anti-diary diary. Harvey Molotch offers some guidance on how to avoid academic narrowness and some suggestions with regard to keeping our imaginations alive and open. Others discuss the social role of writers and intellectuals and the importance of public engagement (Mills, Said, Puwar and Sharma). Mark Carrigan's online resource *Sociological Imagination* offers a good example of the possibilities that are available now to create open platforms for ideas and also create spaces of intellectual dialogue.

Bauman, Zygmunt. (2010) *44 Letters from the Liquid Modern World*. Cambridge: Polity Press.

Bauman, Zygmunt. (2012) *This is Not a Diary*. Cambridge: Polity Press.

Benjamin, Walter. (1973) 'Unpacking My Library', in *Walter Benjamin: Illuminations*, ed. Hannah Arendt. London: Fontana/Collins, pp. 59–67.

Bhabha, Homi. (1995) 'Unpacking My Library Again', *Journal of Midwest Modern Language Association*, 28(1): 5–18.

Eagleton, Terry. (2001) *The Gatekeeper: A Memoir.*
London: Allen Lane/The Penguin Press.

Manguel, Alberto. (1996) *A History of Reading.*
New York: Viking.

Manguel, Alberto. (2006) *The Library at Night.*
New Haven, CT and London: Yale University Press.

Mills, Charles Wright. (1944) 'The Social Role of the
Intellectual', in C. *Wright Mills: Power, Politics and People,*
ed. Irving Horowitz. New York: Ballantine.

Molotch, Harvey. (1994) 'Going Out',
Sociological Forum, 9(2): 221–239.

Patter – Pat Thomson's blog at:
http://patthomson.net/author/patthomson/

Puwar, Nirmal and Sharma, Sanjay. (2009) 'Short-Circuiting
Knowledge Production', in *Edu-Factory Collective towards a
Global Autonomous University.*
New York: Autonomedia, pp. 45–49.

Robinson, Katherine. (2015) 'An Everyday Public?: Placing
Public Libraries in London and Berlin', doctoral thesis in the
Department of Sociology, London School of Economics and
Political Science, University of London.

Said, Edward. (1996) *Representations of the Intellectual: the
1993 Reith Lectures.* London: Vintage.

Said, Edward. (2004) *Humanism and Democratic Criticism.*
Basingstoke: Palgrave Macmillan.

Tips, Leads and Follow-Ups

Steegmuller, Francis, ed. (1982) *The Letters of Gustave Flaubert: 1857–1880*.
Cambridge, MA and London: Belknap Press.

The Sociological Imagination website hosted by
Mark Carrigan, at: http://sociologicalimagination.org

Heroes and heroines

There are some books that I need to have close to hand all the time. This list of essential reading, from Primo Levi to Judith Butler, is all in that category. Each has a very individual voice but somehow together they furnish my own imagination and help me get on with the task of writing. There is a diversity of literature here, from poets to philosophers, both ancient and modern, but each of these books is like an inspiring companion. Many of them are mentioned in the diary directly but others are there as invisible encouragements between the lines.

Aeschylus. (1986) 'The Agamemnon', in Edith Hamilton, ed. *Three Greek Plays*. New York and London: W.W. Norton & Company.

Améry, Jean. (1994) *On Aging: Revolt and Resignation*. Bloomington and Indianapolis: Indiana University Press.

Angier, Carole. (2002) *The Double Bond: Primo Levi, a Life*. London: Viking.

Arendt, Hannah. (2005) *Essays in Understanding: 1930–1954: Formation, Exile and Totalitarianism*. New York: Schocken Books.

Baldwin, James. (1953) *Go Tell It On The Mountain*. New York: Alfred Knopf.

Berger, John. (1991) *And Our Faces, My Heart, Brief as Photos*. New York: Vintage International.

Tips, Leads and Follow-Ups

Berger, John. (2006) *Here is Where We Meet.*
London: Bloomsbury Publishing.

Berger, John and Mohr, Jean. (2010) *A Seventh Man: A Book
of Images and Words about the Experience of Migrant Workers in
Europe.* London and New York: Verso.

Bielski, Nella. (2006) *The Year is '42.*
New York: Vintage Books.

Bourdieu, Pierre. (2007) *Sketch for a Self-Analysis.*
Cambridge: Polity Press.

Butler, Judith. (2004) *Precarious Life: The Powers of Mourning
and Violence.* London and New York: Verso.

Calvino, Italo. (1997) *Invisible Cities.* London: Vintage.

Du Bois, W.E.B. (1903) *The Souls of Black Folk.*
New York: Bantam Classic.

Gilroy, Paul. (1987) *'There Ain't No Black in the Union Jack':
The Cultural Politics of Race and Nation.* London: Hutchinson.

Hazlitt, William. (1944) *Selected Essays of William Hazlitt,* ed.
Geoffrey Keynes. London: The Nonesuch Press.

Hebdige, Dick. (1979) *Subculture: The Meaning of Style.*
London: Routledge.

Hoggart, Richard. (1989) 'Introduction', in George Orwell,
The Road to Wigan Pier. London: Penguin, pp. v–xii.

Hoggart, Richard. (1992) *An Imagined Life: Life and Times 1959–91*. London: Chatto & Windus.

Hooks, Bell. (2000) *All About Loving: New Visions*. London: The Women's Press.

Jacobs, Jane. (1961) *The Death and Life of Great American Cities*. New York: Vintage Books.

Levi, Primo. (1991) *Other People's Trades*. London: Abacus.

Lorde, Audre. (2007) *Sister Outsider: Essays and Speeches*. Berkeley, CA: Crossing Press.

Lorenz, Konrad. (1977) *Behind the Mirror: A Search for a Natural History of Human Knowledge*. New York and London: Harcourt Brace Jovanovich.

Moore, Michael. (2004) *The Official Fahrenheit 9/11 Reader*. New York: Simon & Schuster.

Orwell, George. (1990) *Nineteen Eighty-Four*. Oxford: Heinemann Educational.

Perec, Georges. (1997) *Species of Spaces and Other Pieces*. London: Penguin Books.

Sontag, Susan. (2003) *Regarding the Pain of Others*. London: Penguin Books.

Sparberg Alexiou, Alice. (2006) *Jane Jacobs: Urban Visionary*. New Brunswick, NJ and London: Rutgers University Press.

Thomson, Ian. (2002) *Primo Levi*. London: Hutchinson.

Tips, Leads and Follow-Ups

Vallejo, César. (1980) César Vallejo: *The Complete Posthumous Poetry*. Berkeley and London: University of California Press.

Williams, William Carlos. (1984) *The Doctor Stories*.
New York: New Direction Books.

Music as a hinterland

Many of the thinkers I admire have a secret, or semi-secret, life as a musician. This group brings together a diverse range of authors including Roland Barthes, Theodor Adorno, Ernst Bloch, Ralph Ellison, Howard Becker, Stuart Hall, Edward Said and Paul Gilroy. Either explicitly or tacitly, they all enhance their intellectual craft with music. In the same way music – playing the guitar – is the hinterland for my own academic work. I have always had an extra-mural life as a working musician, although in the age of YouTube it is no longer possible to keep such things a secret. I mention it here, albeit reluctantly, because there are recurring references in this book to music and musicians. These sources are listed below, along with others that have enhanced my understanding of the value of thinking with music.

Becker, Howard S. (1963) *Outsiders: Studies in the Sociology of Deviance*. London: Collier Macmillan.

Ellison, Ralph. (2001) *Living with Music: Ralph Ellison's Jazz Writings*. New York: The Modern Library.

Faulkner, Robert R. and Becker, Howard S. (2009) *'Do You Know . . .?' The Jazz Repertoire in Action*. London and Chicago, IL: University of Chicago Press.

Gilroy, Paul. (2003) 'Between the Blues and the Blues Dance', in Michael Bull and Les Back, eds. *The Auditory Cultures Reader*. Oxford: Berg, pp. 381–395.

Tips, Leads and Follow-Ups

Hall, Stuart. (2003) 'The Calypso Kings', in Michael Bull and Les Back, eds. *The Auditory Cultures Reader*. Oxford: Berg, pp. 419–425.

Hesmondhalgh, David. (2013) *Why Music Matters*. Oxford: Wiley Blackwell.

Lees, Gene. (2001) *You Can't Steal a Gift: Dizzy, Clark, Milt and Nat*. Lincoln, NE and London: University of Nebraska Press.

Nussbaum, Martha. (2006) *Frontiers of Justice: Disability, Nationality, Species Membership*. Cambridge, MA and London: Belknap Press.

Richards, Keith. (2010) *Life*. London: Weidenfeld and Nicholson.

Said, Edward. (1991) *Musical Elaborations*. New York: Columbia University Press.

Sennett, Richard. (2003) 'Resistance', in Michael Bull and Les Back, eds. *The Auditory Cultures Reader*. Oxford: Berg, pp. 381–395, pp. 481–484.

Street, John. (2012) *Music and Politics*. Cambridge: Polity.

Sudnow, Philip. (1978) *The Ways of the Hand*. Cambridge, MA: MIT Press.

Wilmer, Val. (1991) *Mama Said There'd Be Days Like This: My Life in the Jazz World*. London: The Women's Press.

Printed in the United States
by Baker & Taylor Publisher Services